THE GREAT BRITISH
BAKE OFF
WINTER KITCHEN

LIZZIE KAMENETZKY

LOVE

Executive producer: Anna Beattie
BBC commissioning executive: Emma Willis
Commissioning editor: Muna Reyal
Project editor: Laura Higginson
Copy editor: Norma Macmillan
Design: Allies Design
Photography: Nassima Rothacker
Food styling: Annie Nichols
Props styling: Polly Webb-Wilson
Production: Helen Everson and Beccy Jones

10 9 8 7 6 5 4 3 2

Published in 2013 by BBC Books, an imprint of Ebury Publishing.
A Random House Group Company.

The Random House Group Limited Reg. No. 954009

Addresses for companies within the Random House Group can be found at
www.randomhouse.co.uk
A CIP catalogue record for this book is available from the
British Library.

ISBN: 978 1 849 90630 2

The Random House Group Limited supports The Forest Stewardship Council
(FSC®), the leading international forest certification organisation. Our books
carrying the FSC label are printed on FSC® certified paper. FSC is the only forest
certification scheme endorsed by the leading environmental organisations, including
Greenpeace. Our paper procurement policy can be found at www.randomhouse.
co.uk/environment

MIX
Paper from
responsible sources
FSC® C016897
www.fsc.org

Colour origination by Altaimage, London.
Printed and bound in the UK by Butler Tanner and Dennis Ltd.

CONTENTS

FOREWORD

It is often said that bakers are givers, but it's not just bakers; anyone who throws a meal together for someone else is doing something generous.

Whether cooking a quick supper for your best friend, putting tea on the table for six toddlers, rustling up a chilli for an army of mates, doing the Sunday roast or feeding the grandchildren on a special occasion, everyone who makes something for someone else to eat does so in the spirit of generosity.

The Great British Bake Off celebrates this generosity – and it celebrates home cooking. So many of the recipes cooked by the Bake Off bakers each year have either been handed down through families, or are staples cooked week in, week out, in homes across the country. Bake Off is as much about the food we bake at home as it is about the show-stopping, extravagant gestures.

Bake Off has, for many, rekindled a passion for creating something from scratch – we witness this process on the show every week. This book of winter feasts builds upon Bake Off's ethos of good food made with love.

It's a fantastic collection of recipes, with something for every day of the week and for all occasions: from cosy soups and starters to impressive show-stopping dinners for friends; from signature dishes that you can serve the family on school nights to fabulous feasts for special occasions. Many of the recipes use seasonal ingredients so there really is no excuse not to make the most of the fantastic range of British ingredients that are available throughout winter.

Mary and Paul might not be watching your every move, but try out these recipes for the winter evenings, and you'll be a star baker in your own home …

Bake Off Team x

INTRODUCTION

Winter isn't something to grumble about. Instead it should be something that is welcomed and celebrated. One of the wonderful things about Britain is our distinct seasons. Think about that perfect spring day in early March when the day feels lighter and fresher, or about when summer first arrives and you throw off your coat and jumper and step out into the sunshine. Or about that day at the end of August, when the morning begins to feels crisper and cooler, a sign that autumn is around the corner and the first frosts of winter are on their way.

We should revel in these changes, and more particularly in eating in sympathy with the seasons, because just as you think you have eaten enough jersey royals or asparagus to last a lifetime, the season moves on, bringing with it fresh delights to savour. *The Great British Bake Off Winter Kitchen* will give you recipes to help you get the most out of this season.

The winter larder is full of bounty, if you know the right places to look. Autumn brings apples and pears, in bucket loads, to be made into sweet cakes and warming puddings or to preserve to eat throughout the winter as chutneys. There are vast arrays of pumpkin and squash in all shapes and sizes. Autumn is the time of the mushroom – while farmed mushrooms are available most of the year, the wild mushroom is a seasonal delicacy.

Citrus fruits come into their own in winter, with limes and lemons being at their peak from tropical climes. It is also the time for juice-filled satsumas, clementines and mandarins; just the smell of peeling a clementine will transport you to Christmas and mid winter. There are also short-lived citrus delights such as blood oranges with their sunset glow and thick-skinned Seville oranges beloved by marmalade makers. Brassicas are the undisputed king of the winter vegetables. Their strength lies in their many varieties, bringing colour and crunch to the winter table.

One final thing: there is an idea that many people hold to be true that cooking is an exact science, that one must follow a recipe to the letter, never deviating even by one degree. But if you were to give the exact same recipe to a room full of people, every single dish would come out different because they would all interpret things in different ways.

When it comes to savoury dishes, a little experimentation should be encouraged, so the recipes in this book offer some latitude. All the essential quantities are given, but for some ingredients it is better to let cooks think for themselves. How much is a splash of cream or a handful of herbs? You decide! Choose according to your personal preference and momentary whim.

A good recipe should work in its entirety, and will have been rigorously put through its paces, but when all is said and done, a recipe can be just a guideline, an idea. Why not switch the herbs around, swap chicken for lamb or pork, try lime zest instead of lemon?

But what about the baking recipes you say, surely there we must have precision? This is true. Sweet recipes are less forgiving than savoury and a certain amount of obedience to the rules is necessary in order for the cake to rise as light as thistledown. However, even here there is room to play. Why not exchange apple for pear, add some dried fruit where previously there was none, some beloved spice or a hint of booze?

The most important thing is to have fun with this book. Love it, cook from it, not just the recipes that first catch your attention, but those that you might not choose on a first flick through. The recipes have been loved, tested and honed, and most importantly devoured by many hungry people. These are recipes for life, ones that you will come back to time and again, and your guide to surviving winter with full and satisfied bellies.

WHITE BEAN, SMOKY BACON ...
BUTTERNUT SQUASH, CHILLI AND
FENNEL SEEDS ... SPICED SWEET
POTATO ... WILD MUSHROOMS ...
LEMONY CHICKEN, ORZO AND
CHARD ... WATERCRESS WITH
CHORIZO CRUMBS

SOUPS

Winter is the right time for soups. Of course we eat them all year round, but there is something about cold weather, wind and rain that makes us want to hunker down with a big bowl of steaming soup.

You can make a soup out of almost anything, so try to be imaginative in your kitchen, using what you have to hand. A good place to start is with an onion. There is something truly appetising about the smell of frying onion – if you have yet to decide what you are going to cook, inspiration is sure to come.

Lentils and pulses make great soups, giving substance and texture. If you have time, soak dried pulses, otherwise use tinned beans or chickpeas, which are great storecupboard ingredients for a soup-maker to have on hand. Try adding some crisp-fried bacon or spicy chorizo, or cooked chicken and ham. Or leave your soup veggie.

Leftovers are another good starting point for a soup. Don't throw away those few roasties or scoops of cauliflower cheese from Sunday lunch, and never, under any circumstances, chuck out any leftover gravy, even if it's just a spoonful or two. They can all be blended with some good stock to make a warming bowlful.

WHITE BEAN, SMOKY BACON AND SAVOY CABBAGE

A really hearty and healthy soup to sustain you through the long winter days. Dried beans have a firmer texture than their tinned counterpart and are less expensive, but if you are short of time you could use 2 x 400g tins of cannellini beans, drained and rinsed – add them to the stew for the final simmering.

SERVES 6–8

250g dried cannellini or other white beans, soaked in cold water overnight

1 litre cold water

1 x 500g piece smoked streaky bacon, cut into chunks, or smoked bacon lardons

2 tablespoons olive oil

1 large onion, chopped

1 large carrot, chopped

3 garlic cloves, finely chopped

500g floury potatoes, peeled and cut into bite-sized pieces

1.5 litres ham or chicken stock

½ large Savoy cabbage, thinly sliced

2 tablespoons finely chopped fresh parsley

salt and black pepper

STEP 1

Put the drained beans in a saucepan and cover with the cold water. Bring to the boil, skimming off any scum as it rises to the surface. Reduce the heat, cover and leave to simmer for 45 minutes until tender. Drain and set aside.

STEP 2

Fry the bacon chunks or lardons in a large deep saucepan over a medium heat for 10–12 minutes until golden and they've released their fat. Remove the bacon with a slotted spoon and set aside. Add the olive oil to the bacon fat in the pan and stir in the onion and carrot. Cook over a low heat for about 15 minutes, stirring occasionally, until softened and starting to colour. Stir in the garlic and cook for a further 2 minutes.

STEP 3

Return the bacon pieces to the pan along with the potatoes and pour over the stock. Bring to the boil, then simmer for 10 minutes. Add the cabbage and cooked beans and season to taste with salt and pepper. Simmer for a further 5–10 minutes until everything is tender. Stir in the parsley and serve in warmed soup bowls with bread, such as the Poppyseed Loaf on page 278.

BUTTERNUT SQUASH WITH CHILLI AND FENNEL SEED

Vegetarian

The tender flesh of butternut squash makes it a perfect candidate for a rich and creamy soup. Try this one served with slices of homemade sourdough (see page 266), toasted and rubbed with a halved garlic clove, then spread with soft goat's cheese or cream cheese and top with a good drizzle of extra-virgin olive oil.

SERVES 6

YOU WILL NEED: A BLENDER OR HAND BLENDER

1kg butternut squash

2 tablespoons rapeseed oil

1–2 red chillies, finely chopped

a knob of unsalted butter

2 large onions, finely chopped

2 garlic cloves, finely chopped

1 tablespoon fennel seeds

1 litre vegetable stock

a good splash of double cream

salt and black pepper

STEP 1

Heat the oven to 200°C/400°F/gas 6. Peel the squash, cut it in half lengthways and scoop out the seeds and fibres, then cut the flesh into wedges. Put the squash wedges in a roasting tin. Drizzle over the oil, season and sprinkle with half the chillies. Turn the squash to coat with the seasoned oil. Place in the oven and roast for about 45 minutes until tender, shaking the tin occasionally so the squash doesn't stick.

STEP 2

Melt the butter in a deep saucepan. Add the onions and garlic and cook over a low heat for about 15 minutes until soft and lightly golden, stirring occasionally. Add the remaining chilli together with the fennel seeds and cook for a further minute.

STEP 3

Add the squash to the saucepan and pour over the stock. Bring to a simmer. Blend it in batches in a blender, or in a pan using a hand blender, until smooth. If you want an extra-smooth soup, pass it through a sieve. Reheat if necessary, then stir in the cream and check the seasoning before serving.

SPICED SWEET POTATO AND COCONUT

Vegetarian

With its natural sweetness and soft texture, the sweet potato cries out to be made into a velvety soup that will warm you from your nose to your toes. The one here is perfect for popping into a flask and taking on a long winter walk, along with some homemade soda bread (see page 259) to tear and dunk.

SERVES 6

YOU WILL NEED: A BLENDER OR HAND BLENDER

2 tablespoons coconut oil

1 large onion, finely chopped

1kg sweet potatoes, peeled and cut into small chunks

500g floury potatoes, peeled and cut into chunks

3 garlic cloves, peeled

2 red chillies

2cm piece of fresh root ginger, peeled

1 cinnamon stick

2 teaspoons ground turmeric

1 teaspoon ground coriander

1 teaspoon ground cumin

1 litre vegetable stock

vegetable oil, for shallow-frying

5 shallots, very finely sliced

flaky sea salt

160ml tinned coconut cream

salt and black pepper

STEP 1

Heat the coconut oil in a large saucepan and gently fry the onion over a medium heat for about 10 minutes until soft. Add the sweet potatoes, potatoes, garlic cloves, whole chillies, ginger and spices and cook for a minute, stirring to coat the vegetables with the spices, allowing their flavours to infuse and develop.

STEP 2

Add enough vegetable stock so it just covers the sweet potato and potato pieces (if necessary, add a little water). Bring to the boil, then cover the pan, reduce the heat and simmer for 25–30 minutes until everything is tender.

STEP 3

Meanwhile, heat a good layer of vegetable oil in a frying pan over a medium heat. Add the shallots and fry for 10–15 minutes until they are deep golden and crisp. Drain on kitchen paper and sprinkle with sea salt.

STEP 4

Remove the chillies, ginger and cinnamon stick from the soup, then blend it in batches in a blender, or in the pan using a hand blender, until smooth. Stir in the coconut cream. Reheat gently over a low heat; season well. Ladle into bowls and top each with a scattering of crispy shallot.

WILD MUSHROOM SOUP

Vegetarian

When wild mushrooms are in season nothing can beat their rich earthy-woody flavour in a proper mushroom soup. At other times of the year you can make this using field mushrooms or a mix of chestnut and white mushrooms – the dried porcini will add a wild 'shroom kick.

SERVES 6

YOU WILL NEED: A BLENDER OR HAND BLENDER

1 thick slice white bread, crusts removed

2–3 tablespoons milk

50g dried porcini mushrooms

80g butter

2 shallots, finely chopped

600g mixed fresh wild mushrooms (such as chanterelles or girolles, ceps, horn of plenty, puffball), sliced

3 garlic cloves, crushed

3–4 sprigs of fresh thyme

1 litre vegetable stock

4 tablespoons finely chopped fresh parsley

freshly grated nutmeg

salt and black pepper

thick double cream, to serve

lemon juice, to finish (optional)

STEP 1

Put the bread on a saucer and drizzle over enough milk to moisten; set aside. Put the porcini in a small bowl and pour over enough boiling water just to cover; leave to soak for 10–15 minutes to rehydrate them.

STEP 2

Melt the butter in a saucepan and cook the shallots over a low heat for 8–10 minutes until soft and translucent. Add the fresh mushrooms, increase the heat and cook, stirring, until the moisture they exude has mostly evaporated. Add the garlic and thyme sprigs and cook for a further minute.

STEP 3

Tear the moistened bread into pieces and add to the pan. Cook, stirring, until the bread has broken down completely. Pour in the stock and the rehydrated porcini with their soaking liquid (leave any grit in the bottom of the bowl). Bring to a simmer, then cook for 10–12 minutes until the mushrooms are very soft.

STEP 4

Stir in 2 tablespoons of the parsley and a grating of nutmeg. Blend the soup in batches in a blender, or in a pan using a hand blender, until smooth. Reheat if necessary. Season to taste, then ladle into warmed bowls or mugs. Serve each topped with a dollop of double cream, a sprinkling of the remaining parsley and a squeeze of lemon to taste. This soup is perfect to serve with the White Rolls on page 260.

LEMONY CHICKEN BROTH WITH ORZO PASTA AND CHARD

Orzo is a little rice-shaped pasta that is great in soups and stews. If you can't find it, any little pasta shape – the smaller the better – would work here: try conchigliette (tiny shells), stelle (little stars) or risoni (like orzo but smaller). Chard lends a rich greenness to the soup – look for slender-stemmed Swiss chard or ruby chard. If the stems are quite robust, slice them and add to the soup a little earlier than the sliced leaves – about halfway through the pasta cooking time. Your soup will have more bulk but will be delicious for it. Small baby chard leaves can just be tossed into the soup whole. If you can't find chard, spinach will lend a similar iron-rich flavour.

SERVES 4

2 tablespoons olive oil

1 red onion, finely sliced

2 garlic cloves, crushed

500ml each chicken stock and water

6 skinless boneless chicken thighs

a few sprigs of fresh thyme

thinly pared zest and juice of 1 lemon

200g orzo pasta

300g chard (see introduction), sliced

salt and black pepper

STEP 1
Heat the oil in a deep saucepan over a medium heat and fry the onion for about 10 minutes until soft. Add the garlic and cook for a further minute, then pour in the chicken stock and water.

STEP 2
Add the chicken thighs, thyme and strips of lemon zest with some salt and pepper. Bring to the boil, then reduce to a simmer and cook for 10–12 minutes until the chicken is just cooked. Remove the chicken thighs with a slotted spoon and set them aside.

STEP 3
Add the orzo pasta to the pan and cook for 6–8 minutes until almost tender. Cut the chicken into chunks and return to the pan with the chard. Cook for a few more minutes until the chard is wilted and tender. Remove from the heat and add the juice of the lemon. Serve immediately.

WATERCRESS SOUP WITH CHORIZO CRUMBS

The natural peppery kick of watercress is softened by cooking into a milder, sweeter flavour that goes perfectly with the oily rich fire of a chorizo crumb. For a more substantial lunchtime meal, add a scattering of crumbled feta cheese and serve with a homemade Watercress and Feta Muffin (see page 255).

SERVES 4

YOU WILL NEED: A BLENDER OR HAND BLENDER

125g spicy cooking chorizo, skinned and chopped

2 tablespoons olive oil, plus extra for drizzling

100g stale sourdough bread, made into crumbs

30g unsalted butter

1 onion, chopped

2 garlic cloves, crushed

1 leek, thinly sliced

1 large, floury potato, such as King Edward, cut into small cubes

1 litre chicken or vegetable stock

500g peppery watercress, roughly chopped plus a few sprigs to garnish

flaky sea salt

double cream, to serve

STEP 1

Heat a frying pan over a high heat, then add the chorizo and cook, stirring, until it is golden brown and crisp. Remove from the pan with a slotted spoon to drain on kitchen paper. When cool enough to handle, crumble the chorizo as small as you can.

STEP 2

Add a little drizzle of olive oil to the frying pan. Add the breadcrumbs and cook over a medium heat, tossing, until golden and crisp. Mix with the crumbled chorizo and season with a little sea salt.

STEP 3

Heat the butter with the 2 tablespoons olive oil in a large saucepan over a medium-low heat. Add the onion, garlic and leek and cook gently for 10–12 minutes until softened. Add the potato and cook for about 5 minutes until it has softened slightly. Pour in the stock, season with sea salt and bring to the boil. Simmer for about 10 minutes until the potato is tender. Add the chopped watercress and stir until just wilted.

STEP 4

Blend in batches in a blender, or in a pan using a hand blender, until smooth. Reheat if necessary, then ladle the hot soup into warm bowls. Add a swirl of double cream to each bowl plus a sprinkling of chorizo crumbs and some extra watercress sprigs.

SPICED PARSNIPS, STICKY CHICKEN ... PORK CHOPS IN CIDER ... ROAST DUCK, BUTTERY POLENTA ... BEETROOT RISOTTO ... STUFFED CHICKEN, BUTTER BEANS ... ROAST PUMPKIN WITH FETA ... QUICK ROAST CHICKEN, CELERIAC MASH ... COD STEW WITH CHICKPEAS ... CREAMY CHEESE, BRUSSEL SPROUT AND ALMOND GRATIN ... OVEN-BAKED RICE ... SAUSAGE AND CHESTNUT PASTA ... MACKEREL, CRISPY CHORIZO ... LAMB-AND-HERB-STUFFED SQUASH ... VEAL STROGANOFF ... SPICE-CRUSTED LAMB FILLET ... STEAK WITH BRAISED LENTILS ... TOMATO-BAKED LAMB WITH OLIVES AND FETA ... SMOKED SAUSAGE AND LENTILS ... HARISSA SALMON WITH LEMONY COUSCOUS

WEEKNIGHT COMFORT

---

*It is all too easy to let mid-week cooking become predictable,
thinking that there isn't enough time to be creative, especially
in the cold winter months when the food we crave seems to
require a lot of effort to make.*

We need to break out of that rut and realise that mid-week meals, even in the
depths of winter, can be simple, easy and – very often – quick to make, while
still being warming and sustaining.

There is no doubt that it can be difficult to find the time and energy after a busy day
to get into the kitchen and start cooking. But there is a secret about many winter
weeknight meals – even though they may take time to cook, there is almost
always very little actual hands-on work.

In this chapter the dishes are either quick – on the table within half an hour –
or simple, with the lion's share of the work being done by the oven or hob.
But they are all hearty and winter-proof.

BENGALI SPICED PARSNIPS WITH STICKY CHICKEN

The spices used here, which are the constituent parts of Bengali five spice or panch phoron, *blend together to form a rounded whole without the flavours of the individual spices being lost.*

SERVES 4

5–6 parsnips, quartered lengthways
  (or cut into sixths if large)

2 red onions, cut into thin wedges

2 teaspoons nigella seeds

2 teaspoons cumin seeds

2 teaspoons fenugreek seeds

2 teaspoons fennel seeds

2 teaspoons black mustard seeds

4 tablespoons olive oil

4 boneless chicken breasts (skin on)

2 tablespoons runny honey

salt and black pepper

chopped fresh coriander, to garnish

STEP 1
Heat the oven to 200°C/400°F/gas 6. Par-cook the parsnips in a pan of boiling salted water for 6 minutes. Drain well, then place in a roasting tin with the red onion wedges.

STEP 2
Toast the spices in a dry frying pan over a low heat until they start to smell fragrant. Remove the pan from the heat.

STEP 3
Drizzle 2 tablespoons of the olive oil over the vegetables, then sprinkle with the toasted spices. Place in the heated oven and roast for 30 minutes, turning the vegetables over halfway through the cooking time.

STEP 4
Meanwhile, heat the remaining olive oil in the frying pan. Season the chicken with salt and pepper, then place in the pan and fry for about 5 minutes until golden all over.

STEP 5
Arrange the chicken breasts on top of the spiced parsnips and drizzle the honey over them. Return the tin to the oven and roast for about 10 minutes until the chicken is golden brown and crisp and cooked through. Sprinkle with chopped coriander before serving.

PORK CHOPS COOKED IN CIDER, SAGE AND MUSTARD

Pork, apple and sage make up one of those perfect combinations of culinary alchemy, where the flavours blend and enhance one another. This dish may be simple but it is a stunner. Serve it with mashed potato.

SERVES 2

1–2 tablespoons olive oil

2 pork chops

2 knobs of butter

1 onion, finely chopped

2 garlic cloves, crushed

1 eating apple such as Braeburn, peeled and cut into wedges

a small handful of fresh sage leaves, chopped, plus extra whole leaves to garnish

150ml medium dry cider

1 tablespoon grain mustard

a good glug of double cream

salt and black pepper

STEP 1

Heat the oven to 180°C/350°F/gas 4. Heat the oil in a casserole over a medium-high heat. Season the pork chops with salt and pepper, then place in the casserole and brown for a minute or so on each side until they have taken on a lovely golden colour. Remove from the pan and set aside.

STEP 2

Add a knob of butter to the casserole, then gently fry the onion for about 10 minutes until softened. Add the garlic and cook for a further minute, then add the apple wedges and cook until they are beginning to soften and take on some colour.

STEP 3

Return the pork chops to the casserole. Add the chopped sage and pour over the cider. Bring to the boil, then cover with a lid and place in the hot oven. Cook for 15 minutes or until the pork is just cooked.

STEP 4

Meanwhile, melt a knob of butter in a small frying pan and fry some whole sage leaves over a low heat for 30 seconds until just crisp. Remove and drain on kitchen paper.

STEP 5

Using a slotted spoon, remove the pork chops and apples to a serving dish; keep hot. Stir the mustard and cream into the sauce in the casserole and bubble on the hob for about 2 minutes until thickened. Check the seasoning, then spoon over the pork. Garnish with the crisp sage leaves.

ROAST DUCK BREAST WITH BUTTERY POLENTA

For a perfectly cooked, rosy pink duck breast with crisp, golden brown skin, the trick is to be patient – you need to make sure you render the fat slowly. Don't try to rush this process or you will end up with a soft and flabby result.

SERVES 4

4 Gressingham duck breasts

flaky sea salt

4 tablespoons aged balsamic vinegar

2 tablespoons runny honey

a sprig of fresh rosemary

chopped fresh parsley, to garnish

FOR THE POLENTA

450ml full-fat milk

450ml water

200g quick-cook polenta

100g Parmesan cheese, freshly grated, plus extra to serve

60g unsalted butter

salt and black pepper

STEP 1

Heat the oven to 200°C/400°F/gas 6. Score the skin on the duck breasts in a criss-cross pattern. Season them well with sea salt, then place them skin side down in a cold ovenproof frying pan.

STEP 2

Set the pan over a medium-low heat and allow the duck fat to melt out and start to sizzle. Leave to cook for about 10 minutes until the skin is a rich golden brown (drain off the fat if it gets too spitty). Turn the breasts over and briefly sear the meat side, then transfer the pan to the heated oven to roast for 6 minutes.

STEP 3

Meanwhile, pour the milk and water for the polenta into a saucepan and bring to the boil.

STEP 4

Remove the duck breasts to a warm plate and set aside to rest. Pour off all the fat from the frying pan, then set the pan over a medium heat and add the vinegar, honey and rosemary. Bring to a simmer, stirring, to make a glaze. Keep hot.

STEP 5

Pour the polenta into the boiling milk mixture in a steady stream, stirring, then cook over a medium heat, stirring constantly, until the polenta comes to the boil. Turn down the heat to very low and simmer for 1 minute, stirring. Remove from the heat. Season with salt and pepper, then stir in the Parmesan and butter.

STEP 6

Place the duck breasts on warmed plates. Spoon the glaze over the breasts and sprinkle with chopped parsley, then serve with the polenta, along with some wilted greens or buttered spinach and extra Parmesan.

BEETROOT RISOTTO WITH THYME AND PECORINO

Vegetarian

Beetroot transforms this dish from a humble risotto into a work of art, colouring the rice a deep, vivid pink and giving it a nutty, earthy flavour. Pecorino has a lovely tang that offsets the sweetness of the beetroot, although if Parmesan is what you have in your fridge this would also do nicely. Risotto may seem like a labour of love, with all that stirring, but you need to do this in order to release the starch from the rice. That's what gives the risotto its silky texture.

SERVES 4

2 medium beetroots (unpeeled)

2 knobs of butter

1 tablespoon olive oil

2 large shallots, finely sliced

4–5 sprigs of fresh thyme

350g Carnaroli risotto rice

250ml white wine

750ml–1 litre hot vegetable stock

100g baby spinach

a small squeeze of lemon juice

35g pecorino cheese, freshly grated

salt and black pepper

STEP 1

Heat the oven to 200°C/400°F/gas 6. Wrap the beetroots in foil and place in the heated oven to roast for 20–25 minutes until tender to the point of a knife. Remove and leave to cool. Once they are cool enough to handle, peel them and cut into bite-sized cubes.

STEP 2

While the beetroots are cooling, heat a knob of butter with the olive oil in a deep frying pan and gently fry the shallots with the thyme for about 10 minutes until soft. Add the risotto rice and stir for a few minutes until the grains are translucent.

STEP 3

Add the white wine and stir until it has been absorbed by the rice. Season the rice with a good amount of salt. Gradually add the hot stock, a ladleful at a time, cooking and stirring until each addition of stock has been absorbed before adding another ladleful (you may not need all the stock).

STEP 4

When the rice is al dente and almost cooked, gently stir in the baby spinach and beetroot cubes. Remove from the heat and stir in the lemon juice, pecorino, a knob of butter and plenty of black pepper. Cover the pan with a lid and allow to stand for a few minutes before serving.

HERB-AND-CHEESE-STUFFED CHICKEN WITH BUTTER BEANS

The lovely thing about using cream cheese as a stuffing is that it doesn't melt away but keeps the chicken succulent. This makes an indulgent but simple after-work meal, but is also perfect as a Friday night supper with friends.

SERVES 4

150g cream cheese

2 tablespoons freshly grated Parmesan cheese

grated zest of 1 lemon plus a squeeze of juice

2 tablespoons chopped fresh thyme

4 chicken breasts (skin on)

olive oil, for drizzling

FOR THE BEAN STEW

1 tablespoon olive oil

1 large onion, finely sliced

2 garlic cloves, finely chopped

200g streaky bacon rashers, cut across into thin strips

2 x 410g tins butter beans, drained and rinsed

100ml each dry cider and hot chicken stock

a handful of fresh flat-leaf parsley, chopped

3 tablespoons crème fraîche

salt and black pepper

STEP 1

Heat the oven to 200°C/400°F/gas 6. Mix together the cream cheese, Parmesan, lemon zest and juice, and thyme and season well with salt and pepper. Carefully slide your finger between the skin and the meat of one chicken breast to create a pocket (don't completely detach the skin from the breast). Push a quarter of the cheese mix under the skin and spread it out evenly. Repeat with the remaining chicken breasts.

STEP 2

Lay the chicken breasts in a non-stick roasting tin. Drizzle with olive oil and season with salt and pepper. Place in the heated oven and roast for 25–30 minutes until cooked through.

STEP 3

Meanwhile, for the bean stew, heat the olive oil in a pan, add the onion and fry over a medium heat until softened but not coloured. Add the garlic and fry for 1 minute, then add the bacon and fry until it is golden. Stir in the beans and cider. Bring to the boil and bubble over a high heat for about 5 minutes until the liquid has reduced a little and the beans are very tender. Add the hot stock and simmer for a further 2–3 minutes, then stir through the parsley and crème fraîche. Season with salt and pepper.

STEP 4

To serve, pile the beans onto 4 plates and top each with a chicken breast.

ROAST PUMPKIN WITH FETA AND OREGANO

Vegetarian

Pumpkins are the kings of the autumn vegetables. There are so many more types than the chunky pumpkins used to make Hallowe'en lanterns (in fact, these are not good for cooking as they have a high water content and tend to be a little flavourless). Look out for culinary pumpkins (as they are sometimes called in supermarkets), or use a squash instead, as these have a dense flesh and sweet flavour.

SERVES 4

2 small pumpkins or squashes such as kabocha, onion, acorn or butternut, 1–1.5kg in total

olive oil, for drizzling

1 bulb of garlic, cloves separated but unpeeled

1 teaspoon crushed dried chilli

picked leaves from 4–5 sprigs of fresh oregano

150g feta cheese, crumbled

50g walnut halves

100g salad leaves

FOR THE DRESSING

2 tablespoons sherry vinegar

pinch of caster sugar

6 tablespoons extra-virgin olive oil

salt and black pepper

STEP 1
Heat the oven to 200°C/400°F/gas 6. Cut the pumpkins or squashes in half and remove the seeds and fibres, then cut into wedges (you can peel the pumpkins or squashes first if you want, although the roasted skins have loads of flavour and give good texture to the salad). Tip into a roasting tin and add a little olive oil, the unpeeled garlic cloves, chilli flakes and oregano. Season well with salt and pepper. Tumble around so everything is coated with seasoned oil, then place in the heated oven and roast for about 30 minutes until tender.

STEP 2
Meanwhile, make a dressing by whisking the sherry vinegar with the sugar and some salt and pepper, then whisking in the extra-virgin olive oil.

STEP 3
When the pumpkin is cooked, drizzle the dressing over the wedges. Spoon onto a serving plate. Add the feta, walnuts and salad leaves, and toss together, then serve.

QUICK ROAST CHICKEN WITH BUTTERY POTATO AND CELERIAC MASH

Nothing is more comforting than a generous helping of roast chicken with creamy mash. This quick version will hit the spot midweek when roasting a whole chicken would take too much time. Celeriac, with its hints of celery and parsley, is a great addition to the mash, but you could also use a couple of parsnips instead, which will give a sweeter result.

SERVES 4

12 shallots

500g floury potatoes, peeled and cut into large chunks

1 small celeriac, peeled and cut into chunks slightly smaller than the potatoes

olive oil, for frying and roasting

4 chicken legs

75g unsalted butter

75ml double cream

freshly grated nutmeg

1–2 tablespoons plain flour

a small glass of dry white wine

350ml chicken stock

picked leaves from a handful of fresh tarragon

salt and black pepper

STEP 1

Heat the oven to 200°C/400°F/gas 6. Put the shallots in a bowl and cover them with boiling water. Leave to stand for 5 minutes, then drain and peel. (The hot water softens the skins and makes it much easier to peel them off.) Set the shallots aside.

STEP 2

Put the potatoes and celeriac in a pan of cold salted water. Bring to the boil, then simmer very gently for about 15 minutes until tender to the point of a sharp knife.

STEP 3

Meanwhile, put the shallots in a roasting tin and drizzle over a little oil. Place in the heated oven and roast for 10 minutes. While the shallots are roasting, heat a little oil in a frying pan. Season the chicken legs with salt and pepper, then place in the pan skin side down. Fry over a medium heat for 4–5 minutes until the skin starts to become crisp.

STEP 4

Using tongs, transfer the chicken legs to the roasting tin, placing them among the shallots. Add another drizzle of oil, then return the tin to the oven and roast for 20–25 minutes until the chicken legs are golden and cooked through.

STEP 5

Drain the potatoes and celeriac and return to the pan. Add the butter and cream and mash well. Season with a good grating of nutmeg and salt and pepper to taste. Keep hot.

STEP 6

Remove the chicken legs and shallots to a plate, cover with foil and leave to rest while you make a quick gravy. Stir the flour (1–2 tablespoons, depending on how thick you like your gravy) into the fat in the roasting tin. Set it over a low heat and cook for 1–2 minutes, stirring, until lightly browned. Add the wine and stir well, then leave to bubble until reduced by half.

STEP 7

Stir in the stock and tarragon and season with salt and pepper to taste. Bring to the boil again and cook for a couple of minutes. Serve the chicken with the mash, shallots and gravy.

SPANISH COD STEW WITH CHICKPEAS

A classic combination of rich spicy chorizo with tender chickpeas and flaky cod. For something a bit more special to serve to friends, you could use salt cod or baccalau, *which has a firm, silky texture. Soak it overnight before cooking.*

SERVES 4

1 tablespoon olive oil

120g sliced cooking chorizo

1 large onion, chopped

2 teaspoons hot smoked paprika

2 teaspoons sweet smoked paprika

a good pinch of crushed dried chillies

100ml red wine

1 x 400g tin chopped tomatoes

2 tablespoons chopped fresh oregano

300ml water

a good pinch of caster sugar

200g tinned chickpeas (drained weight), rinsed

500g skinless sustainable cod fillet, cut into large pieces

a handful of chopped fresh flat-leaf parsley

salt and black pepper

STEP 1
Heat the oil in a large frying pan and fry the chorizo over a medium heat for 3–4 minutes until just starting to become crisp. Remove with a slotted spoon to a bowl and set aside.

STEP 2
Add the onion to the pan along with the hot and sweet paprikas and the chilli flakes. Cook for 8–10 minutes until softened, stirring occasionally. Add the red wine, tomatoes, oregano, water and sugar. Season with salt and pepper. Bring to a simmer and cook for 20 minutes.

STEP 3
Return the chorizo to the pan and add the chickpeas and the pieces of cod. Bubble gently for 3–4 minutes until the cod is just cooked. Taste and add more seasoning, if needed. Sprinkle with the parsley and serve.

CREAMY CHEESE, BRUSSELS SPROUT AND ALMOND GRATIN

Vegetarian

Sprouts are not just for Christmas. Cooked like this, smothered in a silky, rich cheese sauce, they can give cauliflower or leeks a run for their money. This dish is seriously moreish and satisfying, ideal for warming you up on a cold, dark winter night.

SERVES 4–6

500g waxy potatoes, peeled and cut into sprout-sized cubes

600g Brussels sprouts

150g light blue cheese, such as Cashel blue or Dorset blue, crumbled or chopped

200ml double cream

200ml full-fat milk

1 tablespoon grain mustard

50g ground almonds

75g fresh white breadcrumbs

30g Parmesan cheese, freshly grated

salt and black pepper

STEP 1
Heat the oven to 180°C/350°F/gas 4. Par-boil the potatoes in boiling salted water for 6–8 minutes until almost tender, adding the sprouts for the final 2 minutes of cooking. Drain and tumble into a well-buttered ovenproof dish.

STEP 2
In a jug, combine the blue cheese, cream, milk, mustard and almonds. Season well with salt and pepper. Pour the mixture evenly over the sprouts and potatoes.

STEP 3
Mix together the breadcrumbs and Parmesan and scatter over the top. Place in the heated oven and bake for 25–30 minutes until golden and bubbling. Serve hot.

OVEN-BAKED RICE WITH BACON AND WILD MUSHROOMS

In the autumn if you can get your hands on fresh wild mushrooms such as porcini (ceps) or chanterelles you can use these instead of the dried mushrooms. Simply fry them in a little butter before adding to the rice.

SERVES 4

50g dried porcini mushrooms

a good knob of butter

2 tablespoons olive oil

1 onion, finely chopped

2 garlic cloves, finely chopped

1 red chilli, deseeded and finely chopped

200g streaky bacon rashers, cut across into strips

300g basmati rice

200g winter greens such as kale, chard or cavolo nero, thinly sliced

600ml hot chicken or vegetable stock

100g goat's cheese log, crumbled

salt and black pepper

STEP 1

Heat the oven to 180°C/350°F/gas 4. Put the porcini into a small bowl, cover with boiling water and set aside to soak for 10–15 minutes to rehydrate them.

STEP 2

Heat the butter with the olive oil in a medium flameproof casserole and gently fry the onion for about 10 minutes until softened. Add the garlic and chilli and fry for a further minute. Stir in the bacon and cook until it is just starting to become crisp. Add the rice and stir to coat with the buttery juices.

STEP 3

Drain the porcini (reserve the soaking liquid) and chop. Add to the casserole. Pour in the soaking liquid, leaving any sediment at the bottom of the bowl, then add the greens and hot stock. Season with salt and pepper.

STEP 4

Bring to a simmer, then cover the casserole and place it in the heated oven. Bake for 20–25 minutes until all the liquid has been absorbed and the rice is cooked. Fluff up with a fork and stir through the goat's cheese. Serve hot.

SAUSAGE AND CHESTNUT PASTA BAKE

Pasta bakes are perfect when you are short of time but want something tasty and filling at the end of a long day. Fusilli is great for capturing all the creamy sauce in its curls, but you can replace it with any short pasta shape you like.

SERVES 4

500g fusilli pasta

3 tablespoons olive oil

1 onion, finely chopped

2 garlic cloves, finely chopped

400g good quality pork sausages

200g cooked chestnuts

300ml hot chicken stock

250g mascarpone

a small bunch of fresh flat-leaf parsley, finely chopped

a good squeeze of lemon juice

25g Parmesan cheese, freshly grated

salt and black pepper

STEP 1

Bring a large pan of salted water to the boil. Add the pasta and cook for slightly less time than given on the packet, until not quite al dente. Drain and return to the pan. Add 1 tablespoon of the oil and a splash of water, and toss with the pasta (this will stop it sticking together).

STEP 2

Heat the oven to 180°C/350°F/gas 4. Heat the remaining 2 tablespoons oil in a frying pan and cook the onion over a low heat for about 10 minutes until softened. Stir in the garlic and cook for a further minute or so.

STEP 3

Split open the sausages and add the meat to the onion. Fry gently, breaking up the sausage meat with a wooden spoon, for about 5 minutes until golden. Add the chestnuts, stock and mascarpone and season well with salt and pepper. Bubble for a couple of minutes, then stir in the chopped parsley and lemon juice.

STEP 4

Mix the pasta with the sausage and mascarpone sauce and spoon into a gratin or ovenproof dish. Sprinkle the Parmesan over the top. Place in the heated oven and bake for about 20 minutes until bubbling and golden. Serve hot.

MACKEREL AND CRISPY CHORIZO SALAD WITH CELERIAC AND APPLE

With their iridescent skin and firm sweet flesh, mackerel are a great choice when you want something quick yet tasty. This dish is the antidote to winter, being fresh and crunchy with zesty flavours and the clean taste of the sea from the little fillets of fish.

SERVES 4

½ celeriac, peeled

3 eating apples such as Braeburn, peeled and cored

2 tablespoons cider vinegar

a pinch of caster sugar

4 tablespoons olive oil

2 tablespoons crème fraîche

200g cured chorizo, sliced

4 sustainable mackerel, filleted

50g wild rocket leaves

salt and black pepper

STEP 1
Cut the celeriac and the apples into very fine matchsticks. Place in a serving bowl.

STEP 2
Whisk the vinegar with the sugar and some salt and pepper in a small bowl, then whisk in the olive oil and crème fraîche. Pour this dressing over the celeriac and apples and toss well.

STEP 3
Fry the chorizo in a frying pan over a medium heat until crisp. Remove from the pan with a slotted spoon and drain on kitchen paper.

STEP 4
Drain most of the fat from the pan, then return the pan to the heat. Season the mackerel fillets with salt and pepper. Place in the pan skin side down and fry for 2–3 minutes until the skin is crisp. Flip the fillets over and fry briefly on the other side until the fish is just cooked. Serve the warm mackerel with the rocket leaves and celeriac salad sprinkled with chorizo slices.

SPICY LAMB-AND-HERB-STUFFED SQUASH

Autumn brings with it an array of brightly coloured, sweetly flavoured squashes that cry out to be roasted. Small round varieties, such as acorn or onion, are perfect for stuffing. If all you can find is a couple of chunky butternut squashes, simply slice off their bulbous ends, just before they start to widen, then cut each in half around the middle to create 2 squash bowls. You can save the rest of the squash for other dishes.

SERVES 4

2 small round squash, such as acorn or onion, about 500g each

1–2 tablespoons olive oil, plus extra for drizzling

1 red onion, finely sliced

3 garlic cloves, crushed

2 chillies, deseeded and finely chopped

500g lamb mince

2 teaspoons ground allspice

2 teaspoons cumin seeds

1 cinnamon stick

250ml hot chicken stock

1 tablespoon runny honey

50g pine nuts, toasted

a large handful of fresh flat-leaf parsley, chopped, plus extra to garnish

a large handful of fresh coriander, chopped

salt and black pepper

STEP 1

Heat the oven to 200°C/400°F/gas 6. Cut each squash widthways in half and scoop out the seeds and fibres. Place the 4 halves, cut side up, on a baking sheet. Drizzle over some olive oil and season with salt and pepper. Place in the heated oven and roast for 25–30 minutes until tender.

STEP 2

Meanwhile, heat 1–2 tablespoons olive oil in a frying pan over a medium heat and fry the onion for 5–10 minutes until softened. Add the garlic and chillies and fry for a further minute. Add the lamb mince to the pan, increase the heat and fry, breaking the mince up with a wooden spoon, until it is crumbly and browned.

STEP 3

Add the spices and fry for a couple of minutes, then pour in the stock. Add the honey and season with salt and pepper. Stir well. Simmer for about 15 minutes until the stock has evaporated and the lamb mixture is sticky.

STEP 4

Remove the cinnamon stick and stir in the pine nuts and chopped herbs. Spoon the lamb mixture into the cooked squash halves and serve.

VEAL STROGANOFF WITH NOODLES

There has long been a stigma attached to eating veal, but today the standards for producing British rose veal are among the highest in Europe. Veal is very tender with a sweet flavour and makes a good alternative to beef in this otherwise classic stroganoff.

SERVES 4

700g veal escalopes

3 tablespoons olive oil

50g unsalted butter, plus extra for the noodles

1 large onion, very thinly sliced

300g button mushrooms, sliced

½ tablespoon hot smoked paprika

½ tablespoon sweet smoked paprika

300g egg noodles

a good slug of brandy (about 75ml)

150ml beef stock

300ml soured cream

2 teaspoons lemon juice

a small handful of fresh parsley leaves, finely chopped

salt and black pepper

STEP 1
Slice the veal into strips and season with salt and pepper. Heat half the oil in a frying pan over a high heat and fry the veal, in batches and adding more oil when needed, until browned all over. As the veal is browned, transfer to a dish.

STEP 2
Melt the butter in the pan and fry the onion over a medium heat until starting to soften. Add the mushrooms and hot and sweet paprikas and stir to mix. Increase the heat and cook for 3–4 minutes until the mushrooms begin to become golden.

STEP 3
Meanwhile, cook the noodles in a pan of boiling salted water for 3–4 minutes, or according to the packet instructions, until tender. Drain, reserving a little of the cooking water. Return to the empty pan and toss with a little butter and the reserved cooking water. Keep hot.

STEP 4
Remove the frying pan from the heat and add the brandy, then return to the heat to bubble away a little, stirring well. Add the stock, bring back to the boil and bubble for a couple of minutes longer, stirring occasionally.

STEP 5
Return the veal and any juices to the mushrooms in the frying pan and add the soured cream. Check the seasoning. As soon as the stroganoff is piping hot, remove from the heat and add the lemon juice and parsley. Serve with the noodles.

SPICE-CRUSTED LAMB FILLET WITH BAKED RICE

Lamb neck fillet is often thought of as being a cut for slow-cooking but it also makes a great quick-cook cut too. Just make sure you keep it pink and it will be tender and flavoursome. The sultanas or raisins in the baked rice add little bites of sweetness that mingle with the simple spices on the lamb with every mouthful.

SERVES 4

1 tablespoon cumin seeds

1 tablespoon coriander seeds

600g lamb neck fillets

vegetable oil, for frying

1 onion, finely chopped

1 garlic clove, crushed

250g basmati rice

a good pinch of crushed dried chillies

1 cinnamon stick

4 green cardamom pods

450ml hot chicken stock

150g plump golden sultanas or raisins

a handful of chopped fresh coriander

salt and black pepper

STEP 1
Heat the oven to 180°C/350°F/gas 4. Roughly crush the cumin and coriander seeds in a pestle and mortar. Mix with plenty of salt and pepper. Press this mixture all over the lamb neck fillets.

STEP 2
Heat a little vegetable oil in a frying pan over a medium-high heat and fry the lamb fillets to brown them all over. Be careful not to burn the spices. Transfer the fillets to a small roasting tin and set aside.

STEP 3
Heat a little oil in a small flameproof casserole and gently fry the onion for about 10 minutes until soft and starting to become golden. Add the garlic, rice, chilli flakes, cinnamon and cardamom and stir for a minute in the oniony oil.

STEP 4
Pour the hot chicken stock over the rice and stir. Season with salt. Cover with a lid or foil and bring to a simmer, then place in the heated oven along with the roasting tin of lamb. Bake for 20 minutes (the lamb will be tender and pink in the centre).

STEP 5
Remove the roasting tin from the oven and leave the lamb to rest for 10 minutes. Stir the sultanas or raisins and chopped coriander through the baked rice, then keep hot. When the lamb has rested, slice it into thick pieces and serve with the spiced rice.

STEAK WITH BRAISED HERBY LENTILS

When you are eating something as simple as a beautifully seared piece of steak, you really want that piece of meat to be the best that it can possibly be. So look out for dry-aged beef – ideally aged for 28 days or more – with a good amount of fat and some marbling through the meat to give it flavour and keep it tender.

SERVES 4

3 tablespoons olive oil, plus extra for the steaks

1 small onion, finely chopped

2 celery sticks, finely diced

3 anchovy fillets, chopped

300g Puy lentils, rinsed

1 fresh bay leaf

2–3 sprigs of fresh thyme

750ml hot chicken stock

2 x 200g sirloin or rump steaks, at room temperature

a large handful of fresh flat-leaf parsley, chopped

a small handful of fresh dill, finely chopped

2 teaspoons Dijon mustard

a squeeze of lemon juice

extra-virgin olive oil, to taste

salt and black pepper

STEP 1

Heat the olive oil in a saucepan over a medium heat. Add the onion and celery and cook, stirring occasionally, for about 10 minutes until they begin to soften. Add the anchovies and cook for a further minute, stirring.

STEP 2

Add the lentils and stir to coat with the oil and cooking juices, then add the bay leaf, thyme and hot stock. Season with salt and pepper. Bring to the boil, then reduce the heat and simmer for about 15 minutes until the lentils are tender but still holding their shape.

STEP 3

While the lentils are simmering, heat a ridged griddle pan or frying pan over a high heat. Rub the steaks with a little olive oil and season with salt and pepper. Place on the smoking hot pan and cook for 1–2 minutes on each side. Transfer to a plate to rest.

STEP 4

Drain off any remaining stock from the lentils and discard the bay leaf and thyme stalks. Stir the chopped herbs, mustard, lemon juice and a good slug of extra-virgin olive oil into the lentils and check the seasoning. Slice the steaks and serve with the lentils and chicory leaves, if you like.

TOMATO-BAKED LAMB WITH ROSEMARY, OLIVES AND FETA

Fresh tomatoes simply don't cut the mustard during the British winter, and it is now that tinned tomatoes really come into their own. Picked and tinned at the height of ripeness, they add a splash of sunshine to the dark winter. Feta and olives are great friends with tomatoes, helping to bring a taste of the Mediterranean to cold days. To mix things up you could also try this with chicken breasts or pork steaks.

SERVES 4

600g lamb leg steaks

2 tablespoons olive oil

1 onion, finely sliced

2 garlic cloves, sliced

2 sprigs of fresh rosemary

150ml white wine

1 x 400g tin chopped tomatoes

1 tablespoon tomato purée

2 teaspoons red wine vinegar

a pinch of caster sugar

80g small black olives, pitted

a good handful of fresh flat-leaf parsley, chopped

200g feta cheese, crumbled

salt and black pepper

STEP 1

Heat the oven to 180°C/350°F/gas 4. Lay the lamb leg steaks between 2 sheets of clingfilm and pound with a rolling pin to flatten slightly. Heat half the oil in a shallow flameproof casserole and brown the lamb steaks on both sides. Remove from the casserole and set aside.

STEP 2

Heat the remaining oil in the casserole and gently fry the onion for about 10 minutes until soft. Add the garlic and rosemary and cook for a further minute. Pour in the white wine and bubble until reduced by half. Add the tomatoes, half a tomato tin of water, the tomato purée, vinegar and sugar. Season with plenty of salt and pepper, then stir well. Bring to a simmer.

STEP 3

Stir in the olives and parsley, then return the lamb steaks to the casserole, tucking them into the sauce. Scatter the feta over the surface. Place in the heated oven and bake for 15–20 minutes until the cheese is golden brown. Serve with rice or crusty bread.

SMOKED SAUSAGE AND CREAMY LENTILS

Saucisse de Morteau is a lip-smackingly juicy smoked sausage from the Jura region of France. It is worth trying to get hold of this sausage if you can because it will really make the dish sing. If you can't find a saucisse de Morteau, *any other large smoked sausage will work.*

SERVES 4–6

700g saucisse de Morteau or other smoked raw
   boiling sausage

2 tablespoons olive oil

50g butter

4 shallots, finely chopped

1 leek, finely sliced

350g Puy lentils

3 fresh bay leaves

200ml dry white wine

500ml hot chicken stock

100ml double cream

a handful of chopped fresh parsley

salt and black pepper

STEP 1

Heat the oven to 150°C/300°F/gas 2. Place the smoked sausage in an ovenproof pan of cold water. Cover the pan with a lid and cook in the heated oven for 40–45 minutes.

STEP 2

Meanwhile, heat the olive oil with the butter in another ovenproof pan and fry the shallots and leek for about 15 minutes until soft but not browned. Add the lentils with the bay leaves and stir to mix. Pour in the wine and stock. Bring to a simmer, then cover and cook in the oven for 20–30 minutes until the lentils are tender.

STEP 3

Remove the lentil pan from the oven and drain the lentils of any excess cooking liquid. Return the lentils to the pan, add the cream and parsley, and season well with salt and pepper. Thickly slice the smoked sausage and serve on a bed of lentils.

ROAST HARISSA SALMON WITH LEMONY GIANT COUSCOUS

Salmon is an oily fish that is packed with flavour, which makes it a great choice for partnering the chilli kick of harissa. Rose harissa has a more fragrant flavour than regular harissa but either would work well here. The beads of giant couscous absorb their lemony dressing, making them little flavour bombs.

SERVES 4

2 tablespoons rose harissa

1 tablespoon coriander seeds, crushed

grated zest and juice of 1 lemon

1 x 600g piece sustainable salmon fillet (skin on)

800ml chicken or vegetable stock

400g giant couscous

a good drizzle of extra-virgin olive oil

a large handful of fresh flat-leaf parsley, chopped

a small handful of fresh mint leaves, chopped

a small handful of fresh coriander, chopped

salt and black pepper

STEP 1

Mix the harissa with the crushed coriander seeds and half the lemon zest. Rub this mixture all over the salmon and lay it on a baking sheet. Leave in a cool place to marinate for 30 minutes (or longer if you have time).

STEP 2

Heat the oven to 170°C/325°F/gas 3. Place the salmon in the heated oven and roast for 10–12 minutes until just cooked through.

STEP 3

Meanwhile, bring the stock to a simmer in a large pan, add the couscous and cook for 6–8 minutes until tender. Drain and tip into a large bowl. Cool slightly, then toss with the remaining lemon zest, the lemon juice, oil and herbs. Season well with salt and pepper. Flake the salmon over the top of the couscous, and serve.

SLOW-ROAST LAMB, RED ONIONS, MARSALA ... PULLED PORK WITH CHIPOTLE ... APPLE-STUFFED PORK BELLY ... ROAST RIB OF BEEF WITH MUSTARD CRUST ... BEEF WELLINGTON ... PORCHETTA ... CHICKEN AND JERUSALEM ARTICHOKE PILAF ... LENTIL AND HARISSA LAMB SALAD ... CASSOULET ... ROAST CHICKEN WITH LEMON, GARLIC AND PANCETTA STUFFING ... CHICKEN TAGINE WITH BULGUR WHEAT ... BREAM WITH SAFFRON-CREAM MUSSELS ... PUMPKIN AND RICOTTA RAVIOLI ... FRESH PASTA DOUGH ... BUTTERNUT SQUASH, CHARD AND RICOTTA LASAGNE ... SEA BASS WITH GINGER AND CHILLI ... STICKY BEEF RIB RAGÙ ... HERB-CRUSTED LAMB WITH POTATOES

WEEKEND FEASTS

Weekends are for spending time with your nearest and dearest.
What better way to show someone you love them than with
a home-cooked feast? This chapter is about big food, sharing
food, bring-it-to-the-table-for-oohs-and-ahs food.

There is an immense sense of satisfaction to be had from watching your friends
enjoying something you have cooked. The moment of silence around the table as
everyone tucks in, too busy eating to utter more than a few appreciative noises:
that is a moment to savour, just for a minute, before diving in yourself.

A word to the cook who's a bit nervous about cooking for others: just relax.
Having gone to all the effort of preparing a meal for your family and friends,
whatever happens, they are going to eat your food and love you for the
time and trouble you've taken.

Try to remember that cooking should be enjoyable. If something happens
that is not 100 per cent part of the plan, just go with it, pretend that is how it
was meant to be. No one will be any the wiser and, you never know, you may
invent something truly magical by mistake!

SLOW-ROAST LAMB WITH RED ONIONS, MARSALA AND ROSEMARY

Roast lamb is a staple of the great British Sunday lunch. Slow-cooking the lamb at a low temperature really shows it off to its best, making the meat wonderfully succulent and shreddable. Cooking it this way also leaves you free to get on with other things while the oven does all the work.

SERVES 6

1 x 2.5kg shoulder of lamb, at room temperature

400ml chicken stock

100ml dry white wine

6 red onions, cut into thin wedges

4–5 sprigs of fresh rosemary

1 bulb of garlic, cloves separated but not peeled

1 tablespoon fennel seeds

200ml Marsala

salt and black pepper

STEP 1

Heat the oven to 160°C/325°F/gas 3. Season the lamb well, then put it in a large roasting tin with 150ml of the stock and the white wine. Place in the heated oven and roast for 2 hours.

STEP 2

Add the onions, rosemary and garlic to the roasting tin, placing them around and under the lamb. Sprinkle over the fennel seeds and add another splash of stock if the tin looks dry. Roast for a further 1½ hours until the lamb is tender.

STEP 3

Transfer the lamb to a warmed platter. Remove the onions and garlic from the tin with a slotted spoon and arrange around the joint. Cover the lamb loosely with foil and set aside to rest while you make the gravy.

STEP 4

Strain the meat juices from the tin into a small pan (spoon off and discard any fat before or after straining). Add the remaining stock and the Marsala, and season with salt and pepper. Bring to a simmer, then cook to reduce to a flavoursome gravy. Serve this with the lamb.

PULLED PORK
WITH CHIPOTLE

Imagine you are outside on a crisp, clear November 5th, biting into a soft white bun filled with sweet and sticky pulled pork while you warm yourself by a bonfire. Delicious! This is the ultimate in lazy cooking, where the minimum of effort results in the most incredible feasting.

SERVES 10–12

YOU WILL NEED: A BLENDER

6 dried chipotle chillies

1 dried ancho chilli

1 x 3kg boned pork shoulder

5 garlic cloves, crushed

75g dark muscovado sugar

5cm piece of fresh root ginger, peeled and grated

2 teaspoons ground ginger

1 tablespoon fennel seeds

1 tablespoon smoked sweet paprika

5 tablespoons vegetable or groundnut oil

200ml cider

salt and black pepper

soft white buns, to serve

STEP 1

Put the dried chillies in a small bowl and cover with hot water. Leave to soak for 15 minutes until rehydrated and softened. Drain, reserving 3 tablespoons of the soaking water.

STEP 2

While the chillies are soaking, lay the pork shoulder skin side up on a chopping board. Use a Stanley knife or scalpel to score the skin finely, cutting through into the fat (or ask your butcher to do this for you). Pat the pork dry with kitchen paper, then place it skin side down in a large dish.

STEP 3

Put the chillies and reserved soaking water in a blender and add the garlic and sugar. Blend until smooth. Tip into a small bowl and mix in the grated and ground ginger, fennel seeds, paprika and oil. Spread this mixture over the meaty side of the pork, making sure you rub it into all the crevasses. Turn the pork over and wipe the skin clean if necessary. Place in the fridge, uncovered, and leave to marinate for at least 3 hours (or overnight if possible).

STEP 4

Heat the oven to 220°C/425°F/gas 7. Season the pork all over with salt and pepper, then set it, skin-side up, in a roasting tin. Place in the heated oven and roast for 30 minutes.

STEP 5

Pour the cider around the pork and cover the tin with foil. Turn the heat down to 110°C/225°F/gas ¼ and leave to cook slowly for 6–7 hours, basting now and then. If you like, you can leave the pork to cook for up to 15 hours.

STEP 6

About 1 hour before you're ready to serve, remove the foil and turn the oven up to 220°C/425°F/gas 7 again, then roast for 30 minutes to crisp the skin. If the skin isn't crisp enough after this, and you are worried about burning the juices in the tin, cut off the skin with the fat, place it on a rack in another roasting tin and return to the oven to continue roasting. Check every 5 minutes or so until it is crisp.

STEP 7

Allow the pork to rest for at least 20 minutes, then use 2 forks to pull the meat apart. Mix with the juices in the tin, then serve with the crisp skin in soft white buns with salad leaves and soured cream, if you like.

APPLE-AND-HERB-STUFFED PORK BELLY

Quinoa makes a great stuffing as it absorbs lots of juices and flavour while not going sticky, which sometimes happens with breadcrumbs. Little chunks of apple and lots of herbs finish off this sumptuous roast.

SERVES 8–10

1 x 3kg piece of pork belly, at room temperature

2 tablespoons flaky sea salt

FOR THE STUFFING

100g quinoa

340ml water

1½ tablespoons olive oil

35g butter

4 banana shallots, finely sliced

2 garlic cloves, crushed

150g watercress, chopped

2 eating apples, peeled and cut into small pieces

finely grated zest of 1 lemon

a squeeze of lemon juice

a large handful of fresh flat-leaf parsley, finely chopped

salt and black pepper

STEP 1

For the stuffing, put the quinoa in a pan with the water and bring to the boil, then simmer for about 20 minutes until all the water has been absorbed and the quinoa is tender. Drain and refresh under cold running water. Set aside in a bowl.

STEP 2

Heat 1 tablespoon of the oil with 25g butter in a frying pan and gently fry the shallots for about 5 minutes until soft. Add the garlic and chopped watercress and fry for a further minute. Tip into the bowl with the cooled quinoa and mix together. Heat the rest of the oil and butter in the pan and fry the apple pieces until they begin to soften and turn golden. Add to the bowl along with the lemon zest and juice and parsley. Season well with salt and pepper.

STEP 3

Heat the oven to 230°C/450°F/gas 8 or as high as it will go. Remove the rib bones from the pork belly and reserve. Lay the belly skin side up on a chopping board and use a Stanley knife or scalpel to score the skin finely, cutting through into the fat (or ask your butcher to do this for you).

STEP 4

Space out 8 pieces of string 45cm long, side by side and parallel to each other, on the worktop. Set the pork belly, skin-side down, on the string (make sure the pieces of string are lying the same way as the scored lines).

STEP 5

Spoon the stuffing down the middle of the belly, then bring up the sides around the stuffing until they meet. Tie tightly into shape with the string. Weigh the joint to calculate the cooking time: allow 25 minutes per 450g, plus 20 minutes. Turn the belly over and rub the sea salt all over the skin.

STEP 6

Lay the reserved rib bones in a roasting tin and set the pork belly on top with the join underneath. Place in the heated oven and roast for 20 minutes. Turn the oven down to 180°C/350°F/gas 4 and roast for the remainder of the calculated cooking time. When cooked, transfer the pork to a warmed platter and leave to rest, uncovered, for 20 minutes before serving.

ROAST RIB OF BEEF WITH MUSTARD CRUST

A rib of beef is probably the most magnificent of all the roasting joints. A meat thermometer is a great help to ensure it is cooked to your taste. If you don't have one, insert a skewer into the thickest part for 30 seconds, then lay the skewer against the inside of your wrist. If the skewer feels cool, the meat is rare; if just warm, it is medium-rare; if hot, it is medium to well done. Remember that the beef will continue cooking while it rests.

SERVES 8–10

1 x 3-rib joint of beef, about 3.5kg, at room temperature

4 teaspoons Dijon mustard

100g fresh white breadcrumbs

2 tablespoons chopped fresh rosemary

leaves picked from 10 sprigs of fresh thyme

300ml red wine

50ml port

500ml beef stock

1 tablespoon grain mustard

5 allspice berries, lightly crushed

1 teaspoon redcurrant jelly

salt and black pepper

STEP 1

Heat the oven to 200°C/400°F/gas 6. Place the beef, fat side up, in a roasting tin and season all over with salt and pepper.

STEP 2

Mix together 3 teaspoons of the Dijon mustard, breadcrumbs, rosemary and thyme in a bowl. Season with salt and pepper. Smear the remaining Dijon mustard over the fat of the beef, then press the crumb mix on to it. Cover the tin with well-oiled foil. Place in the oven and roast for 20 minutes.

STEP 3

Add 150ml of the wine and a good splash of water to the tin, then cover with foil again. Turn down the heat to 180°C/350°F/gas 4 and roast for a further 1 hour, adding a splash of water occasionally if the tin starts to look dry. Take off the foil and roast for a final 20 minutes to brown the crust. Check to see if the meat is cooked (see above). Remove the beef from the tin and leave to rest, loosely covered with foil, for 20 minutes.

STEP 4

Meanwhile, skim most of the fat from the juices in the tin, then place it on the hob. Add the port and remaining wine and bubble for a few minutes. Stir in the stock, the grainy mustard, the allspice and jelly. Bring back to the boil and bubble for 5–10 minutes, stirring in the sticky bits from the base of the tin. Strain into a jug and skim excess fat from the surface. Serve the beef with the gravy.

BEEF WELLINGTON WITH WILD MUSHROOMS

This is a dish for special occasions – a big piece of beef fillet is eye-wateringly expensive, but you are buying it to celebrate something wonderful. So savour every mouthful of juicy meat with the woody mushrooms, rich and creamy pâté and crisp buttery pastry. When you buy your fillet, tell the butcher that you are making Wellington so he will give you a piece that is as even in size as possible. You can sear the beef and make the mushroom mix well in advance, then keep them in the fridge. But make sure you remove the meat from the fridge at least 30 minutes before you assemble your Wellington, otherwise the fillet may not cook in the correct time.

SERVES 6

25g dried porcini mushrooms

vegetable or groundnut oil, for frying

1 x 1–1.2kg piece of aged beef fillet, cut from the thick end of the fillet (try to get as uniform a piece as possible), at room temperature

70g butter

2 small shallots, very finely chopped

2 garlic cloves, very finely chopped

300g mixed fresh cultivated and wild mushrooms (such as field, chestnut, ceps, chanterelles), chopped

leaves picked from 3–4 sprigs of fresh thyme

4 tablespoons Madeira or brandy

plain flour, for dusting

2 x 375g packs all-butter puff pastry, thawed if frozen

1 medium egg, beaten

75g good-quality chicken liver pâté

salt and black pepper

STEP 1
Put the porcini in a small bowl, cover with boiling water and leave to soak for 10 minutes. Meanwhile, heat a little oil in a heavy-based frying pan. Season the beef well with salt and pepper, then sear it over a high heat until browned all over. Set aside to cool.

STEP 2
Drain the porcini and chop finely. Melt the butter in a saucepan over a medium heat and cook the shallots for about 10 minutes until pale golden. Add the garlic and fry for a further minute. Add the mushrooms, porcini and thyme. Increase the heat a little and cook for 15–20 minutes until the mushrooms have softened and their moisture has evaporated.

STEP 3
Add the Madeira and season well with salt and pepper. Turn up the heat and cook until the wine has evaporated. Tip the mushroom mix into a bowl and set aside to cool completely.

STEP 4

Heat the oven, with a baking sheet inside, to
200°C/400°F/gas 6. Roll out one of the packs of
pastry on a lightly floured worktop to a rectangle
about 25 x 30cm and the thickness of a pound
coin. Place the pastry on a baking sheet lined
with baking paper. Brush the edges of the pastry
with beaten egg, then place the seared beef in the
centre. Spread the chicken liver pâté over the top
and sides of the beef, then press the mushroom
mix into the pâté all over.

STEP 5

Roll out the second pack of pastry to a rectangle
that is 4cm wider and longer than the first one.
Drape the pastry over the beef, matching the
edges and corners all round. Press the edges
together, making sure the pastry is pressed snugly
around the beef. Trim the edges to neaten and
crimp them to make sure they hold together.
Brush the Wellington all over with beaten egg (you
can use any pastry trimmings to decorate the top).

STEP 6

Lift the Wellington, on its baking paper, and
place it on the hot baking sheet in the oven. Cook
for about 30 minutes until the pastry is golden
all over (turn the baking sheet around after
20 minutes to make sure the Wellington cooks
evenly). Remove from the oven and set aside to
rest for 10 minutes before serving, with creamy
mash or Gratin Dauphinois (page 164).

PORCHETTA

This Italian roast pork dish demonstrates perfectly how a few simple good-quality ingredients can make something really special. Traditionally, porchetta is allowed to cool and is then sliced very thinly, but it is just as delicious while still warm.

SERVES 10–12

1 x 3.5–4kg piece of boned pork belly, skin scored

25g flaky sea salt

1 tablespoon fennel seeds

2 tablespoons olive oil

1 large onion, finely chopped

4 garlic cloves, finely sliced

250g boneless pork shoulder, finely chopped

leaves picked from 10 sprigs of fresh thyme

leaves picked from 4 sprigs of fresh rosemary, chopped

a good handful of fresh sage leaves, chopped

a small glass of dry white wine

100g chunky sourdough breadcrumbs

50g pine nuts

75g sultanas

salt and black pepper

STEP 1

Lay the pork belly skin side down on a chopping board and rub half the sea salt and half the fennel seeds over the meat. Set aside.

STEP 2

Heat the oil in a frying pan over a medium heat and gently fry the onion for 15 minutes until soft. Add the garlic and cook for a further minute. Add the chopped pork shoulder to the pan, increase the heat a little and cook until the pork is browned all over. Add the herbs and white wine and season with salt and pepper. Cook until the wine has reduced by half. Spoon the mixture into a bowl and mix in the breadcrumbs, pine nuts and sultanas. Leave this stuffing to cool.

STEP 3

Heat the oven to 230°C/450°F/gas 8. Spread the stuffing over the pork belly. Roll up the belly and secure with string (see page 70). Rub the skin with the remaining sea salt and fennel seeds. Set the joint in a roasting tin.

STEP 4

Place in the oven and roast for 15 minutes, then reduce the heat to 150°C/300°F/gas 2 and roast for a further 3 hours. If you want to crisp up the skin, turn the oven back up to 230°C/450°F/gas 8 and cook for a further 15 minutes.

STEP 5

Remove the pork belly from the tin and allow to rest for at least 15 minutes. Serve with any resting juices and those from the tin (skimmed of fat).

WARM CHICKEN AND JERUSALEM ARTICHOKE PILAF

Knobbly jerusalem artichokes aren't actually artichokes – they are, in fact, a relation of the sunflower. In this pilaf, warm fluffy grains of rice envelop the sweet, nutty chunks of artichoke and shreds of juicy chicken.

SERVES 8

1 x 1.6kg chicken

2 lemons

800g jerusalem artichokes, scrubbed and cut into 2–3cm pieces

1–2 tablespoons olive oil, plus extra for drizzling

2 onions, finely chopped

500g long-grain rice, rinsed under cold running water until the water runs clear

1 litre chicken stock

100g winter greens, such as pointed or Savoy cabbage or curly kale, finely shredded

a handful of fresh dill, chopped

a large handful of fresh parsley, chopped

175g blanched (skinned) hazelnuts, toasted and chopped

salt and black pepper

STEP 1

Heat the oven to 200°C/400°F/gas 6. Place the chicken in a roasting tin. Halve one of the lemons and squeeze a little juice over the jerusalem artichokes, then arrange them around the chicken. Push the lemon halves into the cavity in the chicken. Season the bird all over with salt and pepper and add a good drizzle of olive oil.

STEP 2

Place in the heated oven and roast for about 50–60 minutes until the juices from the chicken run clear. Remove from the oven and leave to rest while you cook the rice.

STEP 3

Heat the olive oil in a large saucepan over a medium heat and fry the onions for about 10 minutes until soft and starting to colour. Add the rice to the pan and stir to coat with the oil. Add the stock and season with salt and pepper. Bring to the boil. Reduce the heat to very low, cover the pan and cook for 15 minutes until all the liquid has been absorbed and the rice is tender. Stir in the shredded greens for the last 2–3 minutes of cooking.

STEP 4

Pull the meat from the chicken in shreds, discarding skin and bones. Tip the rice into a large serving bowl and fluff up with a fork. Fold in the chicken along with any resting juices, the artichokes, herbs, nuts and juice from the second lemon to taste. Check the seasoning, then serve.

WARM LENTIL AND HARISSA LAMB SALAD

The days of a salad being something sad and limp at the side of a plate, with a few token pieces of cucumber and tomato, are thankfully long gone. Today's salads are packed full of flavour and texture. The warm salad here, served with spicy lamb steaks, is made with glistening Puy or black beluga lentils.

SERVES 6

6 lamb leg steaks, about 100g each

3 tablespoons rose harissa

750ml chicken stock

300g Puy or beluga lentils, rinsed

2 garlic cloves, crushed

2 tablespoons cider vinegar

a pinch of caster sugar

6 tablespoons extra-virgin olive oil, plus extra
  for drizzling

2 red onions, very finely sliced

juice of ½ lemon, or more to taste

300g baby salad leaves

250g feta cheese, finely sliced

a large handful of fresh flat-leaf parsley, finely chopped

a handful of fresh mint leaves, finely chopped

salt and black pepper

STEP 1
Coat the lamb leg steaks with the rose harissa, then set aside to marinate for 30 minutes.

STEP 2
Pour the stock into a saucepan and bring to the boil. Add the lentils, then reduce the heat and simmer for about 20–25 minutes until tender. Drain and tip into a wide bowl. Leave to cool.

STEP 3
While the lentils are cooking, mix together the garlic, vinegar and sugar in a small bowl with a little salt and pepper. Whisk in the extra-virgin olive oil until smooth and thick. Set this dressing aside. Put the onions in another bowl and toss with the lemon juice and a drizzle of oil; leave for 10 minutes.

STEP 4
Heat a frying pan over a high heat. Add the lamb steaks and cook for 1–2 minutes on each side until well browned but still pink in the middle. Remove from the pan and set aside somewhere warm to rest while you finish the lentils.

STEP 5
Add the onions, salad leaves, feta, parsley, mint and dressing to the lentils and toss gently to mix. Taste and add a bit more lemon juice if you like. Slice the lamb, then add to the lentil salad with any of the resting juices and serve.

CASSOULET

A good cassoulet takes time and devotion but is worth all the effort – when you bring it to the table you'll be as hungry to eat it as everyone else. You can use ready-prepared duck confit or make your own. To do this, mix a handful of salt with some black peppercorns, juniper berries and fresh thyme leaves and sprinkle all over 4 duck legs, then cover and leave overnight. The next day wipe the legs clean, place in a small roasting tin and cover with melted duck or goose fat. Cook in a low oven (100°C/200°F) for 3 hours until tender. Pack the confit in a sterilised jar with the fat. It will keep in the fridge for several weeks.

SERVES 8–10

2 tablespoons olive oil

1 x 150g piece smoked bacon, cut into thick strips, OR 150g bacon lardons

6 Toulouse sausages

1 large onion, finely sliced

1 celery stick, finely sliced

1 carrot, finely diced

3 garlic cloves, finely chopped

500ml dry white wine

1 bouquet garni

1 x 400g tin chopped tomatoes

800ml hot chicken stock

4 confit duck legs (see introduction)

a large handful of fresh flat-leaf parsley, chopped

50g fresh breadcrumbs

salt and black pepper

FOR THE BEANS

500g dried white haricot or cannellini beans, soaked overnight in cold water

1 onion, chopped

1 celery stick, chopped

1 carrot, chopped

2 fresh bay leaves

5 black peppercorns

1 x 300g piece unsmoked bacon (from your butcher)

STEP 1

First, make the beans. Drain the beans and place in a large saucepan with the rest of the ingredients for the beans. Cover with cold water and bring to the boil. Leave to simmer gently for 30 minutes.

STEP 2

Meanwhile, heat the oil in a large flameproof casserole. Add the bacon and fry gently for about 5 minutes until lightly golden; remove with a slotted spoon. Add the sausages to the pot and fry over a medium heat to brown on all sides. Remove and set aside with the bacon.

STEP 3

Add the onion, celery and carrot to the casserole and fry gently for about 10 minutes until soft and translucent. Add the garlic and fry for a further minute. Pour in the white wine, bring to the boil and bubble briskly for 5 minutes until the liquid is reduced by a third.

STEP 4

Heat the oven to 140°C/275°F/gas 1. Drain the beans and discard the chopped vegetables, bay leaves and peppercorns. Thickly slice the unsmoked bacon from the beans and add to the pot along with the beans, sausages and smoked bacon. Add the bouquet garni and tomatoes and pour in the stock. Tuck the duck confit into the cassoulet. Season well with salt and pepper. Bring to the boil, then transfer, uncovered, to the heated oven to cook for 2½ hours.

STEP 5

Remove the casserole from the oven and increase the temperature to 180°C/350°F/gas 4. Stir the parsley into the cassoulet and scatter the breadcrumbs over the surface. Return to the oven and cook for 20–30 minutes until the crumbs are golden. Serve with steamed greens.

ROAST CHICKEN WITH A LEMON, GARLIC AND PANCETTA STUFFING

There is something about the aroma of a roasting chicken that makes everything all right with the world. Many say you cannot have a roast without roast potatoes, but I think what a roast chicken really needs is smooth, creamy mash to soak up all the amazing flavours.

SERVES 6

50g butter, softened

3 garlic cloves, crushed

4 pancetta slices, very finely sliced into strips

3 anchovy fillets, chopped

grated zest of 1 lemon (reserve the lemon)

a handful of fresh flat-leaf parsley, finely chopped

1 x 1.8kg chicken

1 tablespoon plain flour

a small glass of dry white wine

300ml chicken stock

salt and black pepper

STEP 1

Heat the oven to 200°C/400°F/gas 6. In a small bowl, mash the butter with the garlic, pancetta, anchovies, lemon zest and parsley. Season well with salt and pepper.

STEP 2

Untie your chicken if it is trussed. Working from the neck end, slip your fingers under the skin of the breast to separate the skin from the meat. Smear the flavoured butter all over the breast meat, then pat the skin back into place. Tie the legs back together so they don't spring apart when cooking. Halve the zested lemon and push the halves into the cavity of the chicken.

STEP 3

Put the chicken in a roasting tin and season the bird with salt and pepper. Place in the heated oven and roast for 60–70 minutes until the juices run clear; baste the chicken with the juices in the tin halfway through cooking. Remove from the oven and transfer the chicken to a warmed plate to rest for about 20 minutes.

STEP 4

While the bird is resting, make the gravy. Pour off the juices from the tin into a jug and skim off the fat from the top, reserving 2 tablespoons. Put this fat back into the roasting tin and add the flour. Set the tin over a medium heat and cook, stirring, for a minute or two. Pour in the juices from the jug and the wine, bring to the boil and bubble, stirring to scrape up the sticky brown bits from the tin. Pour in the stock and simmer for 10 minutes.

STEP 5

Season the gravy with salt and pepper, then add any juices from the resting chicken. Pour into a warm jug and serve with the chicken.

CHICKEN TAGINE WITH CHEERFUL BULGUR WHEAT

Tagines are named after the cooking pot in which they are traditionally cooked – a ceramic dish with a tall funnel. As a classic tagine cooks the moisture rises and hits the top of the funnel, then falls back into the dish, thus keeping everything beautifully moist. This tagine is packed full of dried fruit flavours and spices, giving a rich taste of the Middle East.

SERVES 4–6

2 tablespoons olive oil

8 chicken thighs (skin on and bone in)

2 red onions, sliced into wedges

2 large garlic cloves, finely sliced

1 tablespoon ras el hanout spice mix

1 cinnamon stick

1 teaspoon ground cumin

400ml hot chicken stock

2 preserved lemons, flesh discarded and peel finely sliced

125g soft dried apricots

125g soft prunes

1 x 400g tin chickpeas, drained and rinsed

a small handful each of fresh coriander and parsley leaves, chopped

salt and black pepper

FOR THE BULGUR WHEAT

300g bulgur wheat, rinsed

600ml fresh chicken stock or water

a handful of golden sultanas

extra-virgin olive oil, for drizzling

seeds from 1 pomegranate

a handful of blanched (skinned) almonds

a small bunch of fresh mint, chopped

juice of ½ lemon

STEP 1
Heat the olive oil in a flameproof casserole over a medium-high heat. Add the chicken thighs and brown all over. Remove them to a bowl.

STEP 2
Tip out all but 1 tablespoon fat from the pan. Add the onions and garlic and cook over a low heat for 10–12 minutes until softened. Stir in the spices, increase the heat to medium and cook, stirring, for a few minutes.

STEP 3
Return the chicken to the casserole. Pour over the stock, then add the preserved lemons, apricots and prunes and stir to mix. Season with salt and pepper. Bring to the boil, then reduce the heat and simmer for 40 minutes until the chicken is very tender and the sauce is reduced and sticky. Add the chickpeas for the final 5 minutes of cooking.

STEP 4

Meanwhile, cook the bulgur wheat. Place the
bulgur in a pan and cover with the stock or water.
Bring to the boil, then simmer gently for about
15 minutes until tender, adding the sultanas for
the final minute. Drain and tip into a serving
bowl. Drizzle with extra-virgin olive oil. Stir in
the pomegranate seeds, almonds, mint and lemon
juice. Season to taste with salt and pepper.

STEP 5

Scatter the herbs over both the tagine and the
bulgur wheat and serve.

BREAM WITH SAFFRON-CREAM MUSSELS AND SCALLOPS

This is a dish to woo your loved ones and impress your friends. Saffron is a strong spice that needs to be used judiciously or it will overpower the other flavours. It is heavenly with seafood, and its warmth here seeps into the rich creamy sauce.

SERVES 4

1kg mussels

a good knob of unsalted butter

2 tablespoons olive oil, plus extra for frying

2 banana shallots OR 4 small shallots, finely chopped

a large pinch of saffron threads

2 tablespoons hot water

2 garlic cloves, crushed

200ml dry white wine

200ml double cream

4 sustainable sea bream fillets, about 150g each

8–12 king scallops, cleaned (with corals)

lemon juice, to taste

2 tablespoons finely chopped fresh chervil or parsley

salt and black pepper

lemon wedges, to serve

STEP 1
Scrub the mussel shells clean and remove any 'beards'. Discard any mussels that do not close when tapped sharply on the worktop.

STEP 2
Melt the butter with the oil in a large saucepan over a medium heat. Add the shallots and fry for about 10 minutes until soft. While the shallots are cooking, soak the saffron in the hot water in a small bowl for 5 minutes.

STEP 3
Add the garlic to the shallots and cook for a further minute. Increase the heat and add the mussels, saffron and white wine. Cover the pan with a tight-fitting lid and cook, carefully shaking the pan occasionally, for 2–3 minutes until the mussel shells open.

STEP 4
Remove from the heat. Lift the mussels from the pan with a slotted spoon; discard any that have not opened. Remove most of the mussels from their shells, keeping a few in shell for garnish. Set all the mussels aside.

STEP 5
Add the cream to the cooking liquor left in the pan and bring back to the boil, then reduce the heat and simmer gently for 4–5 minutes until the sauce will coat the back of a spoon.

STEP 6

Meanwhile, heat a little oil in a non-stick frying
pan over a high heat. Season the fish fillets
with salt and pepper, then fry, skin-side down,
for about 2–3 minutes. Flip over and fry for a
further minute on the other side until just cooked.
Remove from the pan and keep hot.

STEP 7

Toss the scallops in a little olive oil, then fry for
1 minute on each side until golden and just
cooked. Remove from the heat.

STEP 8

Return the shelled mussels to the pan of sauce.
Check the seasoning and add a good squeeze of
lemon juice, to taste. Stir in most of the chervil
or parsley. Divide among 4 large, shallow soup
bowls. Arrange the scallops and mussels in their
shells around the bowls and place a fish fillet on
top of each serving. Sprinkle with the remaining
herbs and serve with lemon wedges plus crusty
bread to mop up the juices.

PUMPKIN AND RICOTTA RAVIOLI WITH SAGE BUTTER

Vegetarian

Plump little parcels filled with creamy sweet pumpkin and drizzled with nutty-brown sage butter might just be one of the best combinations ever. These are made even more delicious by the fact that you can proudly say you made them all yourself. Make the pasta dough in two batches as it will be easier to handle.

SERVES 6–8

YOU WILL NEED: A PASTA MACHINE; A 10CM ROUND PASTRY CUTTER

1 x 600g pumpkin

olive oil, for drizzling

½ teaspoon crushed dried chillies

1 large egg yolk

30g Parmesan cheese, freshly grated, plus extra to serve

60g fresh white breadcrumbs

125g ricotta cheese, crumbled

2 x quantities Fresh Pasta Dough (see pages 94–95)

plain flour and semolina flour, for dusting

150g unsalted butter

leaves picked from a small bunch of fresh sage

a squeeze of lemon juice

salt and black pepper

STEP 1

Heat the oven to 200°C/400°F/gas 6. Cut the pumpkin in half and remove the seeds and fibres, then cut into wedges. Put them in a roasting tin and drizzle over some olive oil. Sprinkle with the chilli flakes and season with salt and pepper. Place in the heated oven and roast for 30–35 minutes until the squash is tender. Remove from the oven and leave to cool a little.

STEP 2

Scoop the flesh from the pumpkin wedges into a bowl and mash. Stir in the egg yolk, Parmesan and breadcrumbs. Season well with salt and pepper, then carefully fold in the crumbled ricotta (you want to incorporate it but still have bits of ricotta rather than a smooth mixture).

STEP 3

Using a pasta machine, roll out the pasta dough, a quarter of each batch at a time, to make a very thin pasta sheet about 45cm long and 12cm wide. As you roll each sheet, lay it on a floured worktop and cover with a clean, damp tea towel.

STEP 4

Lay one of the pasta sheets on the worktop in front of you. Spoon 4 heaped tablespoons of the pumpkin filling, evenly spaced, down the middle of the sheet. Brush the edges of the sheet with water, then lay a second sheet of pasta on top, matching the corners. Press together to seal, squeezing out any air bubbles.

STEP 5

Using a 10cm plain round pastry cutter, cut out 4 circles, ensuring the mound of filling is in the centre of each. Transfer the ravioli to a baking sheet dusted with semolina flour and cover with a clean, damp tea towel.

STEP 6

Repeat with the other 6 sheets of pasta and filling to make 16 ravioli in all. (They can be made up to a day in advance and kept in the fridge, in a single layer, until you are ready to cook them.)

STEP 7

Bring a large pan of salted water to the boil, then keep it boiling while you make the sage butter. Melt the butter in a small pan until it starts to foam, add the sage leaves and fry for about 10–20 seconds; remove from the heat and add the lemon juice.

STEP 8

Cook the ravioli in the boiling salted water for 3 minutes. Lift out with a slotted spoon and drain briefly on kitchen paper, then serve with the sage butter and extra Parmesan.

FRESH PASTA DOUGH

Making your own fresh egg pasta dough is seriously satisfying. When it comes snaking its way out of the pasta machine, wafer thin and golden, it will make you smile in anticipation. Fresh egg pasta is best used for filled pasta shapes such as ravioli and tortellini, but you can also use it in your lasagnes or turn it into tagliatelle or pappardelle.

MAKES ABOUT 500G

YOU WILL NEED: A PASTA MACHINE (DEPENDING ON THE SHAPE OF PASTA YOU ARE MAKING)

300g type '00' flour, plus extra for dusting

a good pinch of salt

3 medium eggs plus 1 yolk

2 tablespoons olive oil

semolina flour, for dusting (optional)

STEP 1
Sift the flour and salt onto a clean worktop to form a mound. Make a large well in the centre of the mound. Crack the whole eggs into a jug, add the extra yolk and the olive oil and whisk to combine. Pour the mixture into the well.

STEP 2
Using your fingers, gradually incorporate the flour into the egg mixture, making circular stirring motions and bringing increasing amounts of flour into the centre of the mound. Mix until the ingredients have come together into a soft, kneadable dough (you may not need to incorporate all of the flour).

STEP 3
Knead the dough for a couple of minutes until it is smooth and silky, and springy to the touch. If it feels too dry and cracks start to appear in it, add 1–2 tablespoons water and knead for a bit longer. If the dough is too wet and sticky, add a little more flour. Wrap well in clingfilm, then leave to rest in the fridge for 30 minutes.

STEP 4
Now roll out the dough, either by hand on a lightly floured worktop using a thin rolling pin or using a pasta machine. (Rolling by hand is fine for making lasagne sheets, which don't have to be as thin as pasta for filled shapes such as ravioli, but if you want to make a lot of pasta it is worth investing in a pasta machine.)

STEP 5

To use a pasta machine, divide your dough into quarters and put one quarter on a lightly floured worktop. Set the rest aside, covered with a clean, damp cloth to prevent it from drying out. Shape the piece of dough on the worktop into a rough rectangle, flattening it a little with your hands.

STEP 6

Lightly flour the pasta machine rollers, then feed the dough through on the widest setting and out onto the floured worktop. Fold the rolled pasta in half and feed it through the rollers again on the widest setting. Repeat a third time. Then, without folding, continue to feed the sheet of dough through the machine, reducing the width of the rollers each time, until you are on the narrowest setting – the pasta should be thin enough so you can almost see through it. You may need a second pair of hands to help you. (For lasagne sheets, stop before you reach the narrowest setting as you want to have a thicker, more robust pasta for this.)

STEP 7

Cover the sheet of pasta with a clean damp cloth, then repeat the procedure with the remaining pieces of dough. You can then cut your pasta into the shape you desire. For filled pasta, keep it covered with a damp cloth until you cook it; for tagliatelle, pappardelle and other long pasta shapes, toss with a little semolina flour to keep the strands separate.

BUTTERNUT SQUASH, CHARD AND LEMONY RICOTTA LASAGNE

Vegetarian

A generous scoopful of this rich and creamy dish cannot fail to hit the spot. Even the most die-hard carnivore will be happy and satisfied.

SERVES 8–10

YOU WILL NEED: A LARGE OVENPROOF DISH
(ABOUT 2.5 LITRE)

2 small butternut squashes, halved lengthways

2 red onions, cut into thin wedges

1 bulb of garlic, cloves separated but unpeeled

olive oil, for roasting

500g chard

2 large handfuls of fresh flat-leaf parsley, finely
chopped

finely grated zest of 1 lemon

a good squeeze of lemon juice

250g ricotta cheese

1 x quantity Fresh Pasta Dough (see pages 94–95), cut
into 12 lasagne sheets to fit your dish, OR bought
fresh lasagne sheets

50g Parmesan cheese, freshly grated

30g fresh white breadcrumbs

salt and black pepper

FOR THE WHITE SAUCE

60g unsalted butter

60g plain flour

750ml full-fat milk

75g Parmesan cheese, freshly grated

freshly grated nutmeg

STEP 1

Heat the oven to 200°C/400°F/gas 6. Remove the seeds and fibres from the squash halves, then cut into thin wedges. Tumble the squash, onions and garlic cloves into a roasting tin. Add plenty of salt and pepper and a good glug of olive oil, and turn the vegetables with your hands to coat all over. Place in the heated oven and roast for 25–30 minutes until the squash is just tender.

STEP 2

Meanwhile, blanch the chard in boiling water for 30 seconds. Drain and refresh under cold water. Finely shred the chard.

STEP 3

When the vegetables have roasted, remove them from the oven but do not turn the oven off. Squeeze the garlic flesh from the skins into a large bowl. Add the squash, onions, chard, parsley, and lemon zest and juice. Mix everything together thoroughly. Set aside.

STEP 4

For the sauce, melt the butter in a saucepan over a medium heat, add the flour and stir to mix. Cook for a few minutes, stirring, then gradually stir in the milk to make a smooth sauce. Simmer for a couple of minutes, stirring, until thickened. Add the Parmesan and stir until smooth. Season with nutmeg, salt and pepper to taste.

STEP 5

Spread a third of the squash and chard mixture over the base of a very large (2.5 litre) ovenproof dish. Dot with some of the ricotta. Add a layer of lasagne sheets. Spoon over a third of the sauce. Repeat the layers twice, ending with the last of the sauce. Mix the Parmesan with the breadcrumbs and season with salt and pepper. Sprinkle evenly over the surface of the lasagne.

STEP 6

Place in the heated oven and bake for about 35–40 minutes until the top is golden and the lasagne is bubbling around the edges. Serve hot.

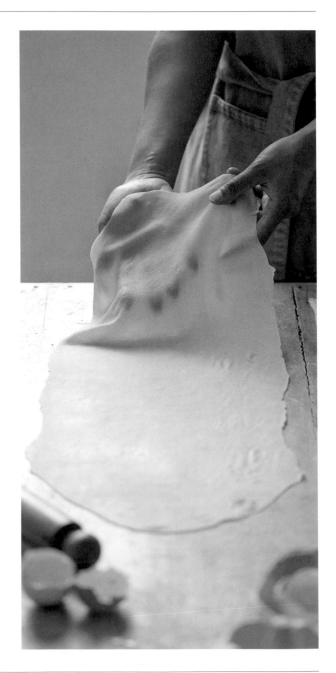

WHOLE BAKED SEA BASS WITH GINGER AND CHILLI

A light, fragrant dish for rainy days, this will lift the spirits and warm the heart. Baking a whole fish can seem daunting but it's really very simple. The parcel enclosing the fish acts as a sort of steamer, keeping the flesh moist and letting all the flavours mingle.

SERVES 4

2 large sustainable sea bass, 800g–1kg each, cleaned and heads removed

3cm piece fresh root ginger, peeled and cut into very thin matchsticks

1–2 red chillies, deseeded and sliced

a bunch of spring onions, green and white parts sliced

2 garlic cloves, finely sliced

2 handfuls of fresh coriander, plus extra chopped coriander to garnish

2 star anise

about 2 teaspoons toasted sesame oil, or to taste

4 tablespoons rice wine

2 tablespoons light soy sauce

2 tablespoons runny honey

juice of 1–2 limes, to taste

salt and black pepper

STEP 1

Heat the oven to 200°C/400°F/gas 6. Cut out 2 rectangular pieces of baking paper, each large enough to wrap a fish. Place a fish in the centre of each piece of paper.

STEP 2

Scatter the ginger, chillies, spring onions and garlic over the fish and fill the cavity of each fish with fresh coriander and a star anise. Bring the long sides of the baking paper up to meet over the fish, then fold up the short ends to form a parcel that is open along the top.

STEP 3

Mix together the sesame oil, rice wine, soy sauce and honey. Drizzle this over the fish, then squeeze the lime juice over them. Season with salt and pepper. Fold the top edges together to seal.

STEP 4

Set the 2 parcels on a baking sheet. Place in the heated oven and bake for about 25 minutes until the fish is cooked through. Serve in the opened parcels, sprinkled with chopped fresh coriander.

STICKY BEEF RIB RAGÙ
WITH TAGLIATELLE

*Beef short ribs are meatier and more tender
than their counterpart of pork spare ribs: a
full slab of beef short ribs measures about
25cm square and has a thick layer of meat and
fat on top of the bones. Each slab normally
contains about 4 ribs, which are cut down
into smaller pieces.*

SERVES 8

3 tablespoons olive oil

3 large onions, finely sliced

4 garlic cloves, finely sliced

2 red chillies, deseeded and finely sliced

100ml dark soy sauce

3 tablespoons runny honey

3 tablespoons maple syrup

3–4 sprigs of fresh thyme

1 x 400g tin chopped tomatoes

2 teaspoons balsamic vinegar

10–12 beef short ribs, each about 12cm long

500g fresh tagliatelle

extra-virgin olive oil, for the tagliatelle

salt and black pepper

STEP 1

Heat the olive oil in a large pan over a medium-
low heat and fry the onions very gently for about
40 minutes until really tender and soft. Add the
garlic and chillies and cook for another couple of
minutes. Add the soy sauce, honey, maple syrup,
thyme, tomatoes and balsamic vinegar and stir to
mix. Simmer for 15–20 minutes until thickened,
stirring occasionally. Season with salt and pepper
and allow to cool.

STEP 2

Put the ribs in a large dish and pour the tomato
mixture over them. Cover and leave to marinate
overnight in a cool place.

STEP 3

Heat the oven to 110°C/225°F/gas ¼. Remove
the ribs from the marinade (reserve the marinade
for later) and place them on a large sheet of foil.
Drizzle a little of the marinade over the ribs,
then wrap up the foil into a parcel and set it on
a baking sheet. Place in the oven and leave to
cook very slowly for 8–9 hours until the meat is
falling from the bone.

STEP 4

Remove the ribs from the foil and spread them
out in a roasting tin. Skim the fat from the meat
juices in the foil, then add to the remaining
reserved marinade. Place the marinade in a pan
and bring to the boil, then simmer to reduce to
a thick gravy consistency.

STEP 5

Increase the oven temperature to 200°C/400°F/
gas 6. Pour the reduced marinade over the ribs
and turn them to coat all over. Place in the oven
and roast for 1 hour, turning the ribs 3 or 4 times.

STEP 6

Remove from the oven. Take the ribs from the tin
and pull the meat from the bones in shreds. Put
into a warmed dish and set aside. Skim any fat
from the sauce in the roasting tin, then set over a
medium-high heat and bring to the boil. Bubble
until slightly reduced and sticky. Stir through the
shredded meat.

STEP 7

Cook the tagliatelle in boiling salted water for
2–3 minutes until just tender; drain and toss with
a little extra-virgin olive oil. Top the pasta with
the slow-cooked beef and serve.

HERB-CRUSTED RACK OF LAMB WITH CHIPPED POTATOES

Racks of lamb are an impressive centrepiece – carve at the table for maximum effect.

SERVES 4–6

800g floury potatoes such as King Edward or Maris Piper, peeled and cut into 2cm cubes

olive oil, for roasting and drizzling

30g fresh white breadcrumbs

finely grated zest of 1 lemon

20g Parmesan cheese, freshly grated

a small handful each of fresh mint and parsley leaves, chopped

2 racks of lamb, about 300g each, trimmed, at room temperature

salt and black pepper

STEP 1

Heat the oven to 220°C/425°F/gas 7. Put the potatoes in a pan of cold salted water, bring to the boil and simmer for a couple of minutes. Drain and return to the pan. Set over a low heat and allow the potatoes to steam dry, tossing them gently to fluff up the edges.

STEP 2

Tip the potatoes into a roasting tin and drizzle over some olive oil. Place in the heated oven and roast for 20 minutes. At the end of this time, reduce the temperature to 200°C/400°F/gas 6.

STEP 3

While the potatoes are roasting, prepare the lamb. Mix together the breadcrumbs, lemon zest, Parmesan and herbs in a bowl. Drizzle in a little olive oil to bind the ingredients together and season well with salt and pepper. Mix with a fork, then set aside.

STEP 4

Heat a little oil in a frying pan over a medium-high heat. Season the lamb, then place in the pan, fat side down, and cook until the fat is golden. Remove from the pan and press the crumb mixture onto the golden fat side to cover evenly.

STEP 5

Toss the potatoes, then place the lamb in the roasting tin with them. Roast for 15–20 minutes for medium-rare lamb. Remove the tin from the oven and cover loosely with foil, then leave to rest for 5 minutes before carving the racks of lamb and serving with the potatoes (and aioli if you have made some; see below).

NOTE

To make an aioli, whisk 2 egg yolks with 2 crushed garlic cloves, 2 teaspoons white wine vinegar and some salt and pepper. Gradually trickle in 200ml mild olive oil, whisking constantly, then slowly whisk in 50–100ml extra-virgin olive oil to make a glossy, thick mayonnaise. Add a good squeeze of lemon juice and check the seasoning. Keep in a cool place until serving.

POT-ROAST CHICKEN ... LAMB MEATBALLS WITH FETA AND CUMIN ... VEAL RAGÙ ... COQ AU VIN ... ALE-BRAISED BEEF WITH WALNUT DUMPLINGS ... LAMB SHANKS WITH GREMOLATA ... PORK BELLY WITH FENNEL AND STICKY RED ONIONS ... PIGS' CHEEKS IN STOUT ... POT-ROAST PHEASANT ... PORK GOULASH WITH GNOCCHI ... PORK SHOULDER WITH LEMON AND GARLIC ... SPICY SAUSAGE AND BEAN CASSEROLE

SLOW COOKING & ONE POTS

There are some dishes that only time can make and these are often the most satisfying things you can cook. Slow-cooked food is simple to prepare and will happily bubble away for hours, filling your kitchen with enticing aromas as you eagerly anticipate what's to come.

Recipes always give an approximate cooking time, but some ingredients – meat in particular – can be stubborn and refuse to cook in the stated timeframe. Patience is the answer, testing every so often until you reach that perfect moment when you can almost cut the meat with a spoon. Use these recipes as a guide, following your intuition and your common sense too.

A great thing about the recipes in this chapter is that they can be made in advance. And they often taste so much better the second time they are cooked to reheat. If you have the weekend ahead of you, cook up one of these dishes on Saturday morning and reheat for supper, or make two at the same time and save one until the next day, letting it mellow overnight.

SPANISH POT-ROAST CHICKEN

The rich colour of this creamy, lightly spiced chicken dish makes it so tempting. Spreading ground almonds under the skin of the chicken keeps the meat moist and gives a sweet, nutty finish to the dish. Try the chicken with a glass of the sherry you've cooked with.

SERVES 6

60g unsalted butter

1 tablespoon smoked paprika

25g ground almonds

1 x 1.8kg chicken

1 lemon, halved

2 tablespoons olive oil

1 large onion, finely sliced

3 garlic cloves, crushed

1 tablespoon plain flour

150ml medium dry sherry, such as palo cortado or manzanilla

500ml hot chicken stock

5–6 sprigs of fresh thyme

3 red peppers, deseeded and sliced

1 x 400g tin butter beans, drained and rinsed

100ml double cream

a handful of fresh tarragon, chopped

salt and black pepper

STEP 1

Heat the oven to 200°C/400°F/gas 6. Mix the butter with the paprika and ground almonds in a bowl. Season with salt and pepper. Untruss the chicken. Working from the neck end, ease the skin away from the breast meat with your fingers. Spread the butter mixture over the breast meat, then smooth the skin back in place. Tie the ends of the legs together to stop them splaying out during cooking.

STEP 2

Season the chicken inside and out. Squeeze the juice from the lemon into the cavity in the chicken, then put the halves inside.

STEP 3

Heat the olive oil in a large flameproof casserole over a medium-high heat. Add the onion and fry for about 10 minutes until softened. Add the garlic and fry for a further minute. Stir in the flour and cook for a minute, then add the sherry, stirring until smoothly blended. Bubble for a couple of minutes until reduced by half, then add the stock, thyme and red peppers.

STEP 4

Place the chicken in the pot. Bring the liquid back to the boil, then cover the pot and place in the heated oven. Cook for 45 minutes.

STEP 5

Uncover the casserole and stir in the beans. Return to the oven and cook, uncovered, for a further 15–20 minutes until the chicken is golden brown and the juices from the thigh run clear when it is pierced with a skewer.

STEP 6

Remove the chicken to a serving dish, loosely cover with foil and set aside to rest while you make the sauce. Return the casserole to the hob. Skim off any fat from the surface of the cooking liquid, then bubble hard for 5 minutes to reduce a little. Stir in the cream and tarragon, and check the seasoning. Spoon the beans, peppers and sauce around the chicken and serve.

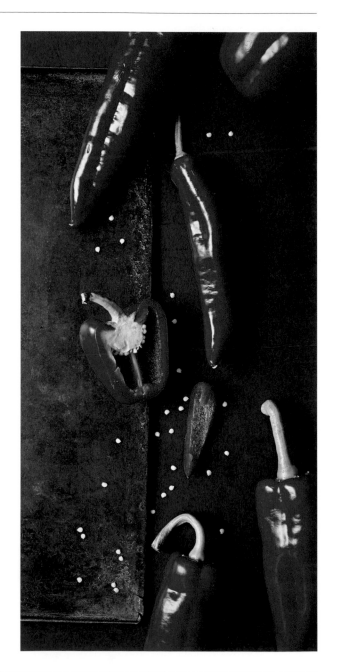

LAMB MEATBALLS WITH FETA AND CUMIN

The meatball may appear humble at first glance but its simplicity is its beauty. Cooked like this, in a sweet and spicy sauce, meatballs make one of the most warming and comforting dishes you could ever wish to eat. Serve with steamed rice – stir a good knob of butter and a little grating of Parmesan cheese into the rice for extra indulgence.

SERVES 6

800g lamb mince

3 garlic cloves, crushed

1 tablespoon freshly ground cumin seeds

200g feta cheese, crumbled

30g toasted pine nuts

a small bunch of fresh mint, finely chopped,
    plus extra to serve

3 tablespoons olive oil, plus extra for your hands

2 onions, finely chopped

2 x 400g tins chopped tomatoes

1 tablespoon runny honey

1–1½ tablespoons rose harissa, to taste

175ml lamb or chicken stock

salt and black pepper

STEP 1

Heat the oven to 190°C/375°F/gas 5. Put the lamb mince in a bowl and add the garlic, cumin, feta, pine nuts and chopped mint. Season with salt and pepper. Mix well with your hands, then shape into about thirty 2.5cm balls with oiled hands.

STEP 2

Heat 2 tablespoons of the olive oil in a flameproof casserole. Add the meatballs, in batches, and fry over a medium-high heat for about 5 minutes until lightly browned on all sides. As each batch is browned, remove with a slotted spoon to a plate.

STEP 3

Add the remaining oil to the casserole and fry the onions gently for 8–10 minutes until soft and lightly golden. Add the tomatoes, honey, rose harissa and stock. Season well with salt and pepper. Stir well, then bring to a simmer.

STEP 4

Drop the meatballs into the sauce then cover and cook in the oven for 20 minutes. Remove the lid and cook for a further 5 minutes or until the sauce is really thick. Sprinkle with extra mint, then serve with steamed rice or couscous.

VEAL RAGÙ

Don't skimp on the cooking time – the longer the ragù bubbles the better. You can always add a splash of stock or water if it thickens too much.

SERVES 6–8

25g dried porcini mushrooms

200ml boiling water

2 tablespoons olive oil

1 x 200g piece pancetta, cut into small lardons

1 large onion, finely chopped

1 carrot, finely diced

2 celery sticks, finely diced

3 garlic cloves, crushed

1 teaspoon fennel seeds

400g good-quality pork sausages, meat removed and crumbled **OR** 400g pork mince

400g British rose veal mince

4–5 big fresh sage leaves, finely chopped

175ml rich red wine

100ml full-fat milk

1 x 400g tin chopped tomatoes

3 tablespoons tomato purée

300ml hot beef stock

salt and black pepper

TO SERVE

500g dried pappardelle

freshly grated Parmesan cheese

STEP 1
Soak the porcini mushrooms in the boiling water for 20 minutes. Drain, reserving the liquid. Finely chop the porcini and set aside.

STEP 2
Heat the oil in a flameproof casserole over a medium heat and fry the pancetta until it is starting to turn golden. Add the onion, carrot and celery and cook for 5 minutes. Add the garlic and fennel seeds and cook for a couple more minutes.

STEP 3
Increase the heat to high. Add the pork sausage meat (or mince) and veal mince with the sage and brown the meat. Add the wine and bubble for a couple of minutes, then add the milk and bubble for few more minutes.

STEP 4
Add the porcini with their soaking liquid, the tomatoes, tomato purée and stock. Season well then bring to the boil, reduce the heat and simmer very gently for 2–2½ hours, stirring occasionally.

STEP 5
When the ragù is nearly ready, cook the dried pappardelle in a pan of boiling salted water according to the packet instructions, until al dente; drain. Serve with the slow-cooked ragù and lots of freshly grated Parmesan.

COQ AU VIN

Some recipes just shouldn't be tinkered with, and a classic like coq au vin is one of those. Traditionally it was made with a cock bird, which can be a little tricky to get hold of these days, but it is worth asking your butcher if he can get you a more mature chicken, as an older bird will give more flavour. Although the wine doesn't have to be the best you own, it is definitely a good idea to use something you would want to drink, because the flavours of the wine are key to the finished dish.

SERVES 4–6

2 tablespoons olive oil

300g bacon lardons

2 tablespoons plain flour

1 x 2kg chicken, jointed into 8 pieces

1 onion, finely chopped

1 large carrot, finely diced

2 celery sticks, finely diced

3 garlic cloves, finely sliced

50ml cognac

1 bottle of full-bodied red wine

400ml chicken stock

1 fresh bay leaf

a few sprigs of fresh thyme

a large knob of butter

12 baby onions OR shallots, peeled and halved if large

200g small button OR chestnut mushrooms, halved

a large handful of fresh flat-leaf parsley, finely chopped

salt and black pepper

STEP 1
Heat the oven to 150°C/300°F/gas 2. Heat the olive oil in a large flameproof casserole and fry the bacon lardons until they are golden and starting to crisp. Remove the lardons with a slotted spoon to a large dish.

STEP 2
Season the flour with salt and pepper. Toss the chicken pieces in the seasoned flour to coat. Add to the casserole and fry them in the bacon fat/oil, turning, until they are golden brown all over. Lift out the chicken pieces and add to the dish with the cooked bacon.

STEP 3
Add the onion, carrot and celery to the casserole and cook for about 10 minutes until softened and lightly browned. Add the garlic and cook for 30 seconds. Pour in the cognac and wine and stir well to mix in any cooked bits stuck to the base of the dish.

STEP 4

Add the stock, bay leaf and thyme and return the chicken and bacon to the casserole. Bring just to the boil, then cover the dish and cook in the heated oven for 40-45 minutes until the chicken is really tender but not falling off the bone.

STEP 5

While the chicken is starting to cook, heat the butter in a frying pan and fry the baby onions or shallots until they are golden all over. Add the mushrooms and fry them until lightly browned. Add these to the casserole and continue to cook the chicken until it is ready.

STEP 6

Remove the chicken pieces with a slotted spoon and keep warm. Simmer the liquid vigorously on the hob for 20–25 minutes until reduced to a glossy sauce. Check the seasoning. Return the chicken to the sauce to warm through again. Sprinkle with the chopped parsley, then serve with creamy mash.

ALE-BRAISED SHIN OF BEEF WITH WALNUT DUMPLINGS

Lifting the lid of a casserole dish to see fluffy golden dumplings peeking out of a rich hearty sauce of braised meats is one of the joys of winter cooking. Beef shin makes the most unctuous braise, because the meat has an almost gelatinous quality.

SERVES 6

25g plain flour

1.2kg boned beef shin, cut into chunks

3–4 tablespoons olive oil

1 small onion, very finely chopped

2 celery sticks, finely chopped

1 carrot, finely chopped

150g chestnut mushrooms, finely chopped

5 garlic cloves, crushed

a small bunch of fresh thyme

2 large fresh bay leaves

450ml brown ale

300ml beef stock

2 tablespoons Worcestershire sauce

a good knob of butter

15 shallots, peeled

salt and black pepper

FOR THE DUMPLINGS

80g self-raising flour

20g finely ground walnuts

1/4 teaspoon salt

50g shredded suet or butter

a handful of fresh flat-leaf parsley, finely chopped

2–3 tablespoons water

STEP 1

Heat the oven to 160°C/325°F/gas 3. Season the flour with salt and pepper and use to coat the chunks of beef. Heat 2 tablespoons of the olive oil in a large flameproof casserole and fry the beef, in batches, over a medium heat until browned all over, adding more oil when necessary. As each batch of beef is browned, lift it out with a slotted spoon and set aside.

STEP 2

Heat another tablespoon of olive oil in the casserole and gently fry the onion, celery and carrot for about 10 minutes until softened. Add the mushrooms and fry until all the moisture from them has evaporated. Add the garlic and fry for a further minute or so.

STEP 3

Return the browned beef to the pot along with the thyme and bay leaves. Pour in the ale, stock and Worcestershire sauce. Bring to the boil, then cover with a lid and transfer to the heated oven. Cook for 2½–3 hours until the beef is really tender and falling apart.

STEP 4

Towards the end of the cooking time, make the dumplings. Put the flour, walnuts, salt, suet and parsley in a bowl. Mix well together. Add enough water to bind to a soft dough. Shape the dough into 9–10 small balls and set aside.

STEP 5

Heat the knob of butter in a frying pan and gently fry the shallots until golden. Remove from the heat.

STEP 6

Remove the casserole from the oven and stir in the shallots. Drop the dumplings evenly on top of the stew. Put the lid back on and return to the oven to cook for a further 20 minutes until the dumplings are puffy and cooked through. Check the seasoning before serving.

LAMB SHANKS WITH WHITE WINE AND GREMOLATA

Lamb shanks are ideal for slow cooking. They are meaty, so although this recipe suggests you serve one shank per person, if you were to strip the meat from the bones into the sauce it could serve 8 people easily. A herby gremolata adds a fresh finish to this hearty dish.

SERVES 6

olive oil, for frying

6 lamb shanks

1 large onion, finely sliced

1 celery stick, finely chopped

2 garlic cloves, finely sliced

500ml white wine

300ml hot lamb or chicken stock

2 fresh bay leaves

4 sprigs of fresh rosemary

a knob of unsalted butter

salt and black pepper

FOR THE GREMOLATA

a large handful of fresh flat-leaf parsley, chopped

finely grated zest of 1 lemon

1 fat garlic clove, crushed

extra-virgin olive oil, to bind

STEP 1

Heat the oven to 160°C/325°F/gas 3. Heat a glug of olive oil in a large flameproof casserole over a medium heat. Season the lamb shanks with salt and pepper, then add to the pot and brown all over. Remove and set aside.

STEP 2

Heat a little more oil in the casserole and fry the onion and celery over a gentle heat for about 10 minutes until really soft and beginning to colour. Add the garlic and fry for a further minute.

STEP 3

Return the lamb shanks to the casserole and pour in the wine and stock. Season well with salt and pepper, and add the bay leaves and rosemary. Bring to the boil, then cover with the lid. Cook in the oven for $2\frac{1}{2}$ –3 hours, turning the shanks over halfway through, until the meat is falling from the bone.

STEP 4

Remove the lamb shanks to a warmed serving dish, cover with foil and keep warm. Discard the bay leaves and rosemary stalks from the casserole. Bring the sauce to the boil on the hob and reduce it by half until it's nice and glossy. Whisk in the butter. Return the lamb shanks to the pot.

STEP 5

Make the gremolata by mixing together the parsley, lemon zest and garlic with enough extra-virgin olive oil to bind them together. Season with salt and pepper. Scatter the gremolata over the lamb shanks and serve with mashed potato.

PORK BELLY WITH FENNEL AND ROASTED STICKY RED ONIONS

Pork belly has to be one of the all-time best roasting joints. Its high fat content keeps it juicy and tender, so it's never dry, even after hours of cooking. And the crackling you get is out of this world.

SERVES 6–8

1 x 3kg piece of pork belly

1 tablespoon flaky sea salt

2 tablespoons fennel seeds

6 red onions, cut into wedges

olive oil, for drizzling

10 sprigs of fresh thyme

½ teaspoon crushed dried chillies

1 tablespoon light soft brown sugar

1 tablespoon cider vinegar

STEP 1

Heat the oven to its highest temperature (230°C/450°F/gas 8). Remove the rib bones from the pork belly; reserve the bones. Lay the belly skin side up on a chopping board and use a Stanley knife or scalpel to score the skin, making the cuts across about 5–10mm apart and cutting through into the fat (or ask your butcher to do this for you). Set aside.

STEP 2

In a pestle and mortar, roughly crush the sea salt with the fennel seeds. Rub this mix all over the pork. Lay the rib bones in the middle of a roasting tin and set the pork belly skin side up on top. Roast for 30 minutes, then reduce the oven temperature to 140°C/275°F/gas 1 and roast for a further 4–5 hours until tender.

STEP 3

About 2 hours before serving, place the onions in a roasting tin and drizzle with oil. Add the thyme and chilli flakes plus a good amount of sea salt. Toss the onion wedges to coat with the oil and seasonings. Place in the oven with the pork and cook for 1 hour.

STEP 4

Add the brown sugar and vinegar to the onions and stir well. Return to the oven and cook for a further hour until sticky and tender. Remove and keep warm.

STEP 5

At the end of the roasting time, if the crackling on the pork isn't as crisp as you'd like, increase the temperature to the highest setting and cook for 15–20 minutes. Allow the pork to rest for 20 minutes before serving with the onions.

PIGS' CHEEKS COOKED IN STOUT

As a cut of meat, cheeks are excellent for slow cooking. They are a hard-working muscle with lots of connective tissue that breaks down when cooked long and slow, leaving the meat so tender you can cut it with a spoon. This recipe would work just as well with beef cheeks – use about 2 cheeks (1kg in total), cut into large pieces.

SERVES 4–6

2 tablespoons plain flour

12 pigs' cheeks (cushion part only, not whole cheeks)

2 tablespoons olive oil, for frying

a knob of unsalted butter

2 large onions, finely sliced

1 leek, finely chopped

1 celery stick, finely chopped

2 garlic cloves, crushed

leaves picked from 5 sprigs of fresh thyme

1 fresh bay leaf

1 tablespoon runny honey

300ml stout

200ml apple juice

salt and black pepper

STEP 1
Heat the oven to 150°C/300°F/gas 2. Season the flour with salt and pepper, then use to coat the pigs' cheeks. Heat 1 tablespoon of the oil in a large flameproof casserole, add the cheeks and cook over a medium heat for 2–3 minutes on each side until browned. Remove and set aside.

STEP 2
Add the remaining oil and the butter to the casserole and gently fry the onions, leek and celery for 15–20 minutes until very soft. Add the garlic, herbs and honey and cook over a medium heat until the vegetables are sticky and golden brown, stirring occasionally.

STEP 3
Return the meat to the casserole. Pour in the stout and apple juice and season well with salt and pepper. Bring to the boil, then cover with the lid and cook in the heated oven for 2½ –3 hours until the meat is very tender.

STEP 4
Remove the cheeks and keep warm. Bring the cooking liquid to the boil on the hob and bubble for about 10–15 minutes until you have a rich sauce. Return the cheeks to the casserole to warm through, then serve immediately.

CREAMY POT-ROAST PHEASANT

Pheasant has the mildest, sweetest flavour of all the game birds, and these days you can easily buy pheasant in most large supermarkets when they are in season. The floral, slightly peppery flavour of juniper berries is great with gamey meats like pheasant.

SERVES 4

50g unsalted butter

2 plump, oven-ready pheasants

100g streaky bacon, chopped

1 large onion, finely chopped

2 celery sticks, finely chopped

2 Cox's apples, peeled and roughly chopped

3 sprigs of fresh thyme

2 fresh bay leaves

12 juniper berries, lightly crushed

150ml Madeira or medium-sweet sherry

150ml chicken stock

125ml crème fraîche

salt and black pepper

STEP 1
Heat the oven to 220°C/425°F/gas 7. Heat half the butter in a large flameproof casserole over a medium-high heat. Season the pheasants inside and out with salt and pepper, then place in the casserole and brown them lightly all over. Lift them out and set aside.

STEP 2
Add the bacon to the pot and fry until it starts to turn golden. Add the onion and celery and fry for a further 5 minutes. Add the apples and fry for 2–3 minutes more.

STEP 3
Return the pheasants to the pot along with the herbs and juniper berries. Pour over the Madeira and stock. Bring to the boil, then cover and transfer to the heated oven. Cook for about 10–15 minutes. Remove the lid and cook for a further 15 minutes.

STEP 4
Remove the casserole from the oven and lift out the pheasants onto a warm serving platter. Set aside to rest. Place the casserole on the hob over a medium heat and add the crème fraiche to the cooking liquid. Stir well and bring to a simmer. Check the seasoning, then serve this sauce with the carved pheasant.

RICH PORK GOULASH WITH GNOCCHI

You might think this dish will be fiery-hot, because it is packed with an array of chillies – from fresh red chilli to hot and smoked paprikas – but the long cooking time and the dollops of soured cream added at the end mellow the heat to a warming glow.

SERVES 4–6

50g lard OR 50ml olive oil

1kg boned pork shoulder, cut into 3cm chunks

2 large onions, sliced

2 garlic cloves, crushed

1 red chilli, finely chopped (optional)

2 tablespoons sweet smoked paprika

2 teaspoons hot smoked paprika

1 teaspoon caraway seeds

½ teaspoon cumin seeds

1 x 400g tin chopped tomatoes

400ml chicken stock

2 tablespoons tomato purée

400g fresh gnocchi

150ml soured cream, plus extra to serve

a small bunch of fresh flat-leaf parsley, chopped

salt and black pepper

STEP 1
Heat the oven to 150°C/300°F/gas 2. Heat the lard or oil in a flameproof casserole, add the pork, in batches, and fry until it is golden brown all over. As each batch of pork is browned, remove with a slotted spoon and set aside.

STEP 2
Add the onions to the casserole and fry for about 10 minutes until golden brown. Add the garlic and chilli and fry for a further minute. Return the pork to the casserole along with the two types of paprika and the caraway and cumin seeds. Season well with salt and pepper. Pour in the tomatoes and stock and add the tomato purée. Stir well. Bring to a simmer, then cover and transfer to the heated oven to cook for about 2 hours until the pork is very tender.

STEP 3
Remove the casserole from the oven and uncover. Leave the goulash to settle, then spoon the excess fat from the surface. While the goulash is settling, cook the gnocchi in a pan of boiling salted water for 1–2 minutes until they just float to the surface; drain well.

STEP 4
Stir the soured cream and parsley into the goulash and serve with the gnocchi, adding a good dollop of extra soured cream to each bowlful.

PORK SHOULDER WITH LEMON AND GARLIC

Pork shoulder makes a great slow-cooked one-pot dish with bags of flavour. Lemon and pork have a particular affinity as the fragrant lemon lifts and cuts through the rich sweet flavour of the meat.

SERVES 8

1 tablespoon olive oil

a knob of unsalted butter

2 red onions, finely sliced

2 lemons

20 fresh sage leaves

1 x 2.5kg boned and rolled pork shoulder joint

2 bulbs of garlic, cloves separated but unpeeled

400ml cider

300ml chicken stock

1 tablespoon Dijon mustard

a good splash of double cream

salt and black pepper

STEP 1

Heat the oven to 220°C/425°F/gas 7. Heat the oil and butter in a deep flameproof casserole over a medium heat and fry the onions for 5 minutes to soften slightly. Add the thinly pared zest of one of the lemons and half the sage leaves and cook for a further minute.

STEP 2

Unroll the pork joint and season well with salt and pepper. Place the remaining sage on the meat, then roll up again and tie into shape. Put the pork in the casserole. Transfer to the heated oven and roast, uncovered, for 30 minutes.

STEP 3

Remove from the oven and turn the heat down to 150°C/300°F/gas 2. Thickly slice the remaining lemon and add to the casserole along with the garlic cloves, cider and stock. Season well with salt and pepper. Cover the casserole with a lid or foil and return to the oven to cook for a further 2½–3 hours, basting the pork regularly with the liquid in the pot.

STEP 4

Lift the pork out of the casserole onto a plate. Loosely cover with foil and set aside to rest. Skim any fat from the liquid in the casserole, then set on the hob and bring to a simmer. Stir in the mustard, double cream and a squeeze of lemon juice. Check the seasoning, adding more salt, pepper and lemon juice to taste. Serve this sauce with the pork, along with rice or potatoes.

SPICY SAUSAGE AND BEAN CASSEROLE

A sausage casserole is perfect winter comfort food – like a crackling fire or a cosy blanket, it wraps you in its warmth. This casserole has an added kick of chilli and smoky chipotle to keep out the winter chills.

SERVES 6

75ml olive oil, plus extra for frying

2 banana shallots OR 4 small shallots, finely sliced

3 garlic cloves, crushed

2 red chillies, finely chopped (deseeded if you like)

2 x 400g tins chopped tomatoes

1–2 tablespoons chipotle chilli paste

200ml red wine

2 tablespoons sherry or red wine vinegar

a good pinch of caster sugar

2 sprigs of fresh rosemary

8 good-quality herby pork sausages

1 x 400g tin butter beans or other white beans, drained and rinsed

a large handful of fresh flat-leaf parsley, chopped

salt and black pepper

STEP 1
Heat the oven to 170°C/325°F/gas 3. Heat the olive oil in a flameproof casserole over a medium-high heat and gently fry the shallots for about 10 minutes until soft. Add the garlic and chillies and cook for a few more minutes.

STEP 2
Pour in the chopped tomatoes and add the chipotle paste, red wine, vinegar, caster sugar and rosemary along with half a tomato tin of water. Season well with salt and pepper. Bring to a simmer, cover and cook in the heated oven for 20 minutes until rich and thick, stirring occasionally. If the sauce starts to thicken too quickly, add a small splash of water.

STEP 3
While the sauce is simmering, heat a little more olive oil in a non-stick frying pan over a medium heat and fry the sausages until browned all over.

STEP 4
Remove the casserole from the oven, stir the beans into the sauce and tuck in the sausages. Cover and return to the oven for a further 20 minutes. Add most of the chopped parsley to the cooked casserole, then serve sprinkled with the rest, with baked potatoes or creamy mash.

FISH PIE ... ROAST CHICKEN
AND STUFFING PIE ... MASHED
POTATO PASTRY ... COTTAGE
PIE WITH A COBBLER TOP ...
GINGER AND CHILLI BEEF PIES
... HOT-WATER CRUST PASTRY ...
CHESTNUT AND MUSHROOM
FILO PIE ... CARAMELISED ONION
TART ... ENRICHED SHORTCRUST
PASTRY ... CHORIZO AND
WATERCRESS TARTLETS ... STEAK
AND ALE PUDDING ... LEEK AND
WENSLEYDALE TART ... WALNUT
PASTRY ... BEEF CHEEK, MUSHROOM
AND MADEIRA PIE ... FLAKY PASTRY
... CRAB AND ROASTED SPRING
ONION TART ... SPINACH AND
GOAT'S CHEESE TART

PIES & TARTS

Whether you're breaking through a golden, crisp pastry crust to release the wonderful aromas of the filling beneath or revelling in the first slice of a richly filled pastry case still warm from the oven, nothing is as fine as a pie or tart.

It is the topping that sets a savoury pie apart from braises and slow cooks. Something wonderful happens under that lid of pastry or potato. You can play around with the pies in this chapter, topping them with other pastries or using mash instead. You could also try turning any of the slow-cooked dishes from the previous chapter into a pie (or the fillings in this chapter into a simple stew or braise).

The word 'tart' covers a wide range of edible delights, both sweet and savoury. In fact, anything consisting of a filling in a pastry case can lay claim to being a tart. Those in this chapter all have savoury fillings, making them ideal for lunch or supper dishes, or starters. The secret to the success of any tart is that, no matter what pastry you choose to use, the case should be crisp, light and flaky. It must be cooked all the way through – no soggy bottoms please!

BEST-EVER FISH PIE

Sometimes simple is best: a fish pie should be rich, smoky and creamy, and made without any fuss. You could also add a couple of sliced hard-boiled eggs and a good handful of wilted watercress or spinach to the filling.

SERVES 6–8

YOU WILL NEED: A 1.5 LITRE OVENPROOF DISH

1kg floury potatoes, peeled and cut into chunks

50g unsalted butter, plus extra for the top

60ml double cream

600g skinless fillet of a firm white fish such as sustainable cod or pollock, cut into large chunks

200g undyed smoked haddock fillet, cut in large chunks

200g peeled large raw king prawns

FOR THE SAUCE

50g unsalted butter

50g plain flour

450ml double cream

1 tablespoon Dijon mustard

a small bunch of fresh dill, finely chopped

a small handful of fresh flat-leaf parsley, finely chopped

salt and black pepper

STEP 1

First make the mash. Cook the potatoes in a pan of boiling salted water for about 12 minutes until tender. Drain well and return to the pan. Set over a low heat to dry them out slightly. Add the butter and cream. When the butter has melted, mash the potatoes and season with plenty of salt and pepper. Set aside.

STEP 2

While the potatoes are cooking, make the sauce. Melt the butter in a saucepan over a medium-low heat. Stir in the flour, then cook, stirring constantly, for 2 minutes. Remove from the heat. Add a little of the cream and stir in briskly until smooth, then return the pan to a low heat. Gradually add the remaining cream, stirring, to make a smooth, thick sauce. Add the Dijon mustard and herbs and season well with salt and pepper. Allow to cool a little.

STEP 3

Heat the oven to 200°C/400°F/gas 6. Put all the fish and prawns in a 1.5 litre ovenproof dish. Pour over the sauce and mix well. Spoon the mashed potato evenly over the top and use a fork to rough up the surface. Dot with butter.

STEP 4

Set the pie dish on a baking sheet (just in case it bubbles over) and place in the heated oven. Bake for 35–40 minutes until it is bubbling underneath the potato and golden brown on top. Serve hot, with buttered peas.

ROAST CHICKEN AND STUFFING PIE WITH MASHED POTATO PASTRY

Possibly the two most comforting dishes combined in one, this roast chicken pie is a masterpiece of a meal. You can make it well in advance, then just pop it in the oven when you are getting ready to eat. You don't have to roast a chicken specially for it – if you have served roast chicken with stuffing balls for Sunday lunch, you could use the leftovers to make this pie for Monday supper.

SERVES 6

YOU WILL NEED: A 1.8 LITRE PIE DISH

30g unsalted butter, softened

1 x 1.8kg chicken

a handful of fresh thyme leaves

1 lemon, cut in half

1 tablespoon plain flour, plus extra for dusting

200ml dry white wine

250ml chicken stock

75ml double cream

1 x quantity Mashed Potato Pastry (see page 136)

1 medium egg, beaten

FOR THE STUFFING BALLS

2 tablespoons olive oil, plus extra for frying

1 small onion, finely chopped

30g fresh white breadcrumbs

200g pork sausage meat

200g pork mince

a large handful of fresh flat-leaf parsley, chopped

10 fresh sage leaves, chopped

salt and black pepper

STEP 1

Heat the oven to 200°C/400°F/gas 6. Smear the soft butter over the skin of the chicken and season well with salt and pepper. Set the bird in a large roasting tin. Tuck the thyme inside the chicken's cavity. Squeeze the lemon juice over the chicken, then push the squeezed lemon halves inside.

STEP 2

Place in the heated oven and roast for about 50 minutes until the juices run clear. Transfer the chicken to a plate to cool. You can turn off the oven for the time being, but don't wash up the roasting tin just yet.

STEP 3

While the chicken is roasting, make the stuffing balls. Heat the olive oil in a frying pan and gently fry the onion for about 10 minutes until soft. Tip into a bowl and add the breadcrumbs, sausage meat and pork mince. Mix together, then add half the parsley and the sage. Season well with salt and pepper. Shape the mixture into walnut-sized balls.

STEP 4

Heat a layer of olive oil in the frying pan and fry the stuffing balls, in batches, until they are golden brown all over. As they are browned, transfer them to a plate, then set aside.

STEP 5

Pour off any juices and all but 1 tablespoon fat from the roasting tin. Set the tin over a low heat, stir in the flour and cook for 1–2 minutes, stirring. Stir in the wine, then bubble until the liquid has reduced by a third. Add the stock and any juices from the resting chicken, then simmer for a couple of minutes. Whisk in the cream and season well with salt and pepper. Set the sauce aside to cool.

STEP 6

Shred the chicken meat (and the crispy skin if you like) and put it in a 1.8 litre pie dish with the stuffing balls. Stir the remaining parsley into the sauce and pour over the chicken and stuffing.

STEP 7

Turn the oven back on to 200°C/400°F/gas 6. Roll out the pastry on a lightly floured worktop to the thickness of a pound coin. Brush the edge of the pie dish with beaten egg, then lay the pastry over the top. Press to seal to the dish, then trim to fit and crimp the edge. Use any trimmings to decorate the top of the pie, if you like. Brush the pastry lid with beaten egg. Place in the heated oven and bake for 30–35 minutes until golden brown. Serve hot.

MASHED POTATO PASTRY

Potato may seem like an odd addition to pastry but it really works. Somehow the pastry turns out crisp yet soft and pillowy, and melts on the tongue when you take a bite. You can use leftover mashed potao or, if you don't have any to hand, bake a large potato instead.

MAKES ENOUGH TO COVER A LARGE PIE DISH

1 large baking potato, about 200g OR 160–170g leftover mashed potato

200g plain flour, plus extra for dusting

a good pinch of salt

125g cold unsalted butter, cubed

1 medium egg yolk

STEP 1

Heat the oven to 200°C/400°F/gas 6. Scrub the baking potato and prick all over with a fork. Place the potato in the heated oven and bake for about 1 hour until tender. Remove from the oven. When cool enough to handle, cut the potato in half and scoop out the flesh into a small bowl. Set aside to cool completely.

STEP 2

Sift the flour and salt into a mixing bowl. Add the butter and rub together with your fingertips until the mixture resembles breadcrumbs (you can also do this in a food processor). Mix in the cooled potato (or leftover mashed potato).

STEP 3

Quickly mix in the egg yolk with a flat-bladed knife until the mixture just starts to come together, then turn out onto a lightly floured worktop and knead briefly. Shape into a disc, wrap in clingfilm and chill for 20–30 minutes before using. (You can keep this pastry in the fridge for 2–3 days or freeze it, wrapped well, for up to 3 months.)

COTTAGE PIE WITH CINNAMON AND MACE AND A BUTTERMILK COBBLER TOP

Instead of the classic mash topping, this pie has a cobbler top – it's just as good as mash for soaking up the juices.

SERVES 6

YOU WILL NEED: A 2.2 LITRE OVENPROOF DISH

2 tablespoons sunflower oil

1 onion, finely chopped

3 garlic cloves, crushed

1 red chilli, deseeded and chopped

1kg good-quality beef mince

1 x 3cm cinnamon stick

2–3 blades of mace

200g chopped tomatoes (fresh or tinned)

1 tablespoon tomato purée

2 teaspoons caster sugar

2 teaspoons red wine vinegar

200ml beef stock

1 tablespoon lemon juice

3 tablespoons chopped fresh coriander

salt and black pepper

FOR THE COBBLER TOPPING

250g plain flour

2 teaspoons baking powder

2 medium eggs, beaten

200ml buttermilk

STEP 1

Heat the oil in a large pan and fry the onion over a low heat for 10 minutes. Add the garlic and fry for a few more minutes. Add the red chilli and fry for 2 minutes, then add the minced beef. Increase the heat and cook for 3–4 minutes, breaking up the meat with a wooden spoon as it browns.

STEP 2

Add the cinnamon stick, mace, tomatoes, tomato purée, sugar, vinegar and stock, and season well with salt and pepper. Simmer, stirring occasionally, for 30 minutes until the liquid has reduced and thickened.

STEP 3

Heat the oven to 200°C/400°F/gas 6. In a bowl, mix together the ingredients for the cobbler topping with some salt and pepper to make a soft dough.

STEP 4

Remove the cinnamon stick and mace from the mince mixture, and stir in the lemon juice and coriander. Check the seasoning, then tip into a 2.2 litre ovenproof dish. Dollop the cobbler mixture all over the top. Place in the heated oven and bake for 30–35 minutes until bubbling hot and the cobbler topping is golden brown. Serve hot.

GINGER AND CHILLI BEEF RAISED PIES

This is a portable pie, a pie for bonfires and eating in the cold crisp air, but it tastes just as delicious enjoyed at the table with creamy mash alongside. The hot-water crust pastry forms a solid shell that encases the filling.

MAKES 6 PIES

YOU WILL NEED: 6 X 220ML METAL PUDDING BASINS

olive oil, for frying and greasing

2 tablespoons plain flour, plus extra for dusting

800g braising steak, cut into 2cm cubes

2 onions, finely chopped

4 garlic cloves, finely chopped

2 red chillies, finely sliced

8cm piece fresh root ginger, peeled and cut into very fine matchsticks

200g shiitake mushrooms, sliced

250ml beef stock

2 star anise

3 tablespoons oyster sauce

3 tablespoons dark soy sauce

a large handful of fresh coriander, chopped

salt and black pepper

FOR THE PASTRY CASES

1 x quantity Hot-water Crust Pastry (see page 141)

1 medium egg, beaten

STEP 1

Heat a thin layer of olive oil in a large flameproof casserole or heavy-based pan over a high heat. Season the flour with salt and pepper, then use to coat the beef. Fry the beef, in batches, until golden all over, adding more oil if necessary. As each batch is browned, remove to a plate. Set aside.

STEP 2

Heat a little more oil in the casserole and reduce the heat, then fry the onions for about 10 minutes until soft but not coloured. Add the garlic, chillies and ginger and cook for a few more minutes. Add the mushrooms and fry until all the liquid they exude has evaporated.

STEP 3

Return the beef to the pot and add the stock, star anise, and oyster and soy sauces. Bring to the boil, then cover and simmer gently for about 1¾ hours until the meat is very tender. Transfer the pie filling to a bowl and cool completely.

STEP 4

Reserve one-third of the pastry for the lids; rewrap this in clingfilm and set aside at room temperature. Divide the remaining pastry into 6 equal pieces. Roll or press out each piece on a lightly floured worktop into a 17cm circle.

Lightly grease 6 x 220ml metal pudding basins with oil. Line each one with a pastry circle, pressing it evenly around the sides and working the pastry up over the edge. Chill, uncovered, in the fridge for 40 minutes to harden.

STEP 6

Heat the oven to 200°C/400°F/gas 6. Stir the coriander into the cooled filling, then divide among the pastry cases. Unwrap the reserved pastry and divide into 6 pieces. Press out each piece to a circle large enough to make a lid for the basins. Make a hole in the centre of the pastry lids (so steam can escape during baking). Dampen the edges of the pastry lids with water, then lay them over the basins and seal all around the edge with your fingers. Crimp the edges and brush the pastry lids with beaten egg.

STEP 7

Set the basins on a baking sheet and place in the heated oven. Bake for about 40 minutes until the pastry is golden and crisp, and the filling is piping hot (cover with foil if the pastry is browning too quickly). Remove from the oven and leave to rest for 5 minutes, then carefully remove the pies from the metal basins.

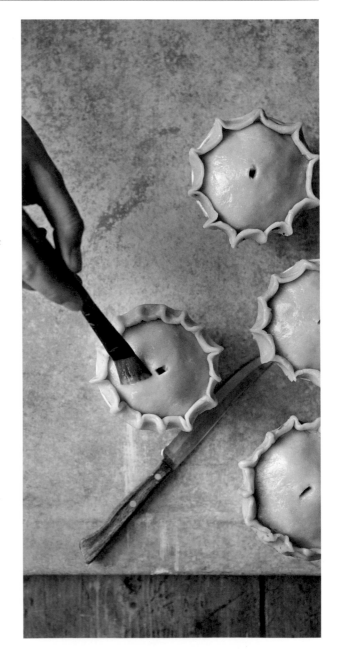

HOT-WATER CRUST PASTRY

Unlike other pastries, hot-water crust is made with flour and a mix of boiling hot fat and water, which results in a tough case for a pie filling. In days past, before refrigeration was invented, hot-water crust pastry wasn't intended to be eaten – it was purely a means of preserving meat fillings. These days the chewy, well-flavoured pastry is as delicious as the pie filling itself.

MAKES ENOUGH FOR 6 INDIVIDUAL PIES

100g unsalted butter, cut into small pieces

100g lard, cut into small pieces

200ml water

500g plain flour

1 teaspoon salt

1 teaspoon icing sugar

1 large egg, beaten

STEP 1

Put the butter, lard and water in a saucepan and bring to a rolling boil, making sure the lard and butter have melted.

STEP 2

Meanwhile, sift the flour, salt and icing sugar into a mixing bowl and make a well in the centre. Add the beaten egg to the well and sprinkle over enough flour to cover the egg.

STEP 3

Pour the boiling mixture around the edge of the flour, then mix quickly with a wooden spoon until combined. Knead briefly into a smooth dough. Use immediately as the pastry will become too firm to use if it gets cold.

CHESTNUT AND MUSHROOM FILO PIE

Vegetarian

A crisp filo case surrounding some of the tastiest winter vegetables. The little pieces of chestnut add a sweet nutty flavour.

SERVES 4–6

YOU WILL NEED: 1 X 20CM SQUARE TIN (4CM DEEP)

150g curly kale or cavalo nero, shredded

150g unsalted butter

olive oil

2 banana shallots, finely sliced

1 large leek, trimmed and sliced

3 garlic cloves, crushed

leaves from a few sprigs of fresh sage, chopped

700g mixed mushrooms, thickly sliced

small glass of dry white wine (about 175ml)

150g cooked, peeled chestnuts, roughly chopped

150ml double cream

juice of ½ lemon

10–12 large sheets of filo pastry

salt and black pepper

STEP 1

Plunge the kale or cavalo nero into a pan of boiling water. Cook for 2 minutes, drain and refresh under cold running water, then squeeze out any excess moisture and set aside.

STEP 2

Melt 40g of the butter with a glug of olive oil in a large, deep frying pan set over a medium heat. Add the shallots and cook for 10 minutes until softened. Add the sliced leek, garlic and sage and cook for a further 3–4 minutes, then add the kale and cook for a minute. Set aside.

STEP 3

Add 15g of butter to the pan with a little oil and cook half the mushrooms over a high heat until the moisture has evaporated. Tip the mushrooms into a bowl, then repeat with the second batch. Return all the mushrooms and veg to the pan. Add the wine and bubble until reduced to about a third. Turn down the heat to medium-low and stir in the chestnuts, cream and lemon juice. Simmer for a few minutes until the sauce has reduced a little. Season and allow to cool.

STEP 4

Melt the remaining butter. Turn on your oven to 190°C/375°F/gas 5 and put in a baking sheet to heat up. Brush a filo sheet with butter and use to line the base and 2 opposite sides of the tin. Butter a second sheet of filo and lay it across the first sheet so the other 2 opposite sides are covered. Continue to layer up, alternating direction, until each side of the tin is covered by 3–4 sheets of filo. Fill the filo case with the mushroom mixture, then fold any excess pastry over the filling. Use the remaining filo, brushed with butter and scrunched, to cover the pie. Place on the hot baking sheet in the heated oven and bake for 35–40 minutes or until the filling is piping hot and the filo pastry is golden.

CARAMELISED ONION TART

Vegetarian

Onions are like the foot soldiers of the vegetable world – they form the base of almost every dish. Rarely do they get a chance to show what they can do. But when cooked long and slow, onions undergo a transformation and become sweet, sticky and tender. This simple but delicious tart really lets the onions shine.

SERVES 6

YOU WILL NEED: A 23CM FLUTED TART TIN

1 tablespoon olive oil

40g butter

4 large Spanish onions, sliced

plain flour, for dusting

1 x quantity Enriched Shortcrust Pastry (see opposite)

2 medium eggs plus 2 egg yolks

325ml double cream

50g Gruyère cheese, finely grated

freshly grated nutmeg

1 tablespoon Dijon mustard

salt and black pepper

STEP 1

Heat the oil and butter in a large sauté pan or frying pan. When the fat is foaming, add the onions and season well with salt and pepper.

Cover with a lid and cook over a very low heat for 30 minutes. Increase the heat a little, remove the lid and cook for a further 15–20 minutes until the onions are very soft and starting to colour and caramelise. Set aside to cool.

STEP 2

While the onions are cooking, roll out the pastry on a lightly floured worktop to the thickness of a pound coin. Use to line a 23cm round, deep, fluted tart tin. Prick the base all over with a fork and chill for 20 minutes.

STEP 3

Heat the oven, with a baking sheet inside, to 200°C/400°F/gas 6. Line the pastry case with baking paper and fill with baking beans or rice. Place on the hot baking sheet in the oven and bake blind for 12 minutes. Remove the paper and beans/rice and return to the oven to bake for a further 5 minutes until golden. Remove from the oven and set aside. Turn the oven down to 180°C/350°F/gas 4.

STEP 4

In a jug, mix the eggs and yolks with the cream and cheese. Season with salt and pepper and plenty of grated nutmeg.

STEP 5

Spread the mustard over the base of the pastry case. Spoon the onions on top. Pour over the cheese and cream mixture. Place in the oven, still on the baking sheet, and bake for 20–30 minutes until the filling is just set. Serve warm or cold.

ENRICHED SHORTCRUST PASTRY

Shortcrust pastry is a staple recipe that any keen cook will want to learn. The keys for success are to rub in the butter quickly and mix lightly so the pastry doesn't get too warm, and to rest the pastry before using so the glutens in the flour can relax. The addition of an egg yolk to a basic shortcrust gives a little extra richness, and adding some sugar turns it into a sweet shortcrust (see page 182). You can also make a deliciously savoury Parmesan pastry (see the variations below).

MAKES ENOUGH TO LINE A 23CM DEEP TART TIN

250g plain flour, plus extra for dusting

½ teaspoon salt

160g cold unsalted butter, diced

1 medium egg yolk

1–2 tablespoons cold water

STEP 1

Sift the flour and salt into a mixing bowl. Rub in the butter with your fingertips until you have a crumble-like mixture.

STEP 2

Add the egg yolk and mix in quickly with a flat-bladed knife, then mix in enough cold water, a little at a time, to bind the mixture into a dough.

STEP 3

Turn out onto a lightly floured worktop. Bring together and knead briefly until smooth, then shape into a disc. Wrap in clingfilm and chill for at least 15 minutes before using.

VARIATIONS

Parmesan Pastry: add 3 tablespoons freshly grated Parmesan cheese to the sifted flour.

Basic Shortcrust Pastry: omit the egg yolk.

Shortcrust Pastry for Mince Pies (makes 12 mince pies): follow the above recipe, but using 170g plain flour and a pinch of salt. Add 75g cubed cold unsalted butter and 25g cubed lard and rub together with your fingertips, as above. Stir in 1 tablespoon caster sugar. Add a large egg yolk and mix in quickly, then add 1–2 tablespoons cold water until you have a dough. Knead and chill as above.

CHORIZO AND WATERCRESS TARTLETS WITH PARMESAN PASTRY

Served with a salad, these make a great weekend lunch for friends. The peppery tang of watercress and the deep red spice of the chorizo are tempered by a creamy filling, and the end result is a satisfying warmth that spreads like a smile.

MAKES 6 TARTLETS

YOU WILL NEED: 8 X 12CM FLUTED TART TINS

1 x quantity Parmesan Pastry (see page 145)

plain flour, for dusting

1 tablespoon olive oil

2 banana shallots OR 4 shallots, finely sliced

250g watercress, finely chopped

200g cooking chorizo, skinned and finely chopped

3 large eggs plus 2 egg yolks

225ml double cream

50g cream cheese

100g Parmesan cheese, freshly grated

salt and black pepper

STEP 1

Heat the oven to 200°C/400°F/gas 6. Divide the pastry into 8 equal pieces. Roll out each piece on a lightly floured worktop and use to line eight 12cm fluted tart tins. Chill for 10 minutes.

STEP 2

Line the pastry cases with baking paper and fill with baking beans or rice. Place in the heated oven and bake blind for 15 minutes. Remove the paper and beans/rice, then bake for a further 5–10 minutes until golden and sandy-feeling to the touch. Remove from the oven and set aside. Reduce the temperature to 180°C/350°F/gas 4.

STEP 3

While the pastry cases are baking, heat the oil in a pan and gently fry the shallots for 5–10 minutes until soft. Add the watercress and cook until just wilted. Transfer the mixture to a bowl. Add the chorizo to the pan and fry over a medium heat, breaking up the meat with a wooden spoon if needed, until cooked and golden brown. Drain on a plate lined with kitchen paper.

STEP 4

In a jug, whisk together the eggs and yolks, cream, cream cheese and Parmesan. Season well with salt and pepper. Add the chorizo to the watercress and mix well, then divide among the pastry cases. Set the tins on a baking sheet and pour the cream mixture into them. Place in the heated oven and bake for 15–20 minutes until the filling is golden and just set.

STEP 5

Cool for 5 minutes before removing the tartlets from the tins. Leave to cool to room temperature. Serve with a crisp winter salad.

STEAK AND ALE PUDDING WITH JUNIPER AND PRUNES

Steamed puddings are not just for those with a sweet tooth. There is something undeniably glorious about puncturing the rich suet crust of a steamed pud, seeing rich, juicy meat flooding out and savouring its aroma.

SERVES 4–6

YOU WILL NEED: A 1.75 LITRE PUDDING BASIN

3 tablespoons plain flour

800g boneless beef shin, cut into large pieces

vegetable oil or beef dripping, for frying

1 medium onion, finely chopped

100ml port

500ml ale

4–5 sprigs of fresh thyme

1 bay leaf

8 juniper berries, lightly crushed

2 star anise

½ tablespoon coriander seeds

350ml beef stock

150g semi-dried prunes, sliced

salt and black pepper

FOR THE PASTRY

400g self-raising flour, plus extra for dusting

200g shredded beef suet

½ teaspoon flaked sea salt

about 300ml cold water

butter, for greasing the basin

STEP 1

Heat the oven to 190°C/375°F/gas 5. Season the flour with salt and pepper, then toss the pieces of beef in the seasoned flour to coat. Heat a good amount of oil or about 25g of dripping in a large frying pan. Add about half the beef and fry over a high heat until well browned all over. Remove the beef with a slotted spoon to a flameproof casserole. Brown the rest of the beef in the same way, adding more oil or fat if necessary, then add to the casserole.

STEP 2

Return the frying pan to the heat and add a little more oil. Add the onion and cook over a medium-low heat, stirring occasionally, for 10 minutes until softened. Pour in the port, stir well and bubble until reduced by half, then add the ale and bring back to the boil. Pour the mixture over the beef in the casserole.

STEP 3

Add the thyme and bay leaf to the pot. Tie the juniper berries, star anise and coriander seeds in a small muslin bag (so you can retrieve it later) and add to the pot along with the beef stock and plenty of salt and pepper. Cover with a lid and bring to a simmer, then transfer to the heated oven and cook for 1 hour.

STEP 4

Remove the lid and continue cooking, stirring occasionally, for a further 30–40 minutes until the beef is tender and the sauce is thick. Remove from the oven and fish out the muslin bag of spices. Check the seasoning, then leave to go cold.

STEP 5

To make the pastry, sift the flour into a bowl and stir in the suet and sea salt. Gradually mix in enough water to make a soft, slightly sticky dough. Turn out onto a floured worktop and bring the dough together into a ball.

STEP 6

Grease a 1.75-litre pudding basin wiht butter. Set aside just under a third of the dough to make the lid for the pudding. Roll out the rest of the dough to 1cm thick and cut out a circle measuring 29cm across. Use this to line the basin, to just below the rim.

STEP 7

Stir the prunes into the cold beef mixture, then spoon into the pastry-lined basin. Brush the edge of the pastry case with water. Roll out the reserved pastry into a circle just large enough to fit into the basin on top of the pastry edge. Place this over the filling. Trim off any excess pastry, then press the edges together well to seal.

STEP 8

Lay a large sheet of foil on top of a sheet of baking paper and fold a pleat in the centre to allow for the pudding to rise. Place, paper side down, over the basin and tie down under the rim with string. Set the pudding basin on an upturned saucer or small trivet (or even a piece of egg box) in a deep saucepan and add enough boiling water in the pan to come halfway up the pudding basin. Cover with a lid and bring the water back to the boil, then reduce the heat so the water is steadily simmering and steam for 2½ hours, adding more water when necessary.

STEP 9

Remove the saucepan from the heat, then carefully lift the basin from the water using oven gloves. Leave it to rest for 5 minutes before cutting off the string and removing the foil and baking paper cover. Run a round-bladed knife around the side of the pudding to loosen it from the basin, then turn out carefully onto a serving plate with a rim to catch the gravy. Serve hot.

LEEK AND WENSLEYDALE TART WITH WALNUT PASTRY

Vegetarian

Wensleydale has a lovely sharp, tangy flavour that comes through in this sweet, creamy leek filling. The walnut pastry sets it off beautifully but you could use a basic or enriched shortcrust instead (see recipes on page 145). The tart is great served still warm from the oven but equally delicious cold the next day.

SERVES 6

YOU WILL NEED: A 30 X 20 X 3CM LOOSE-BOTTOMED FLUTED TART TIN

1 x quantity Walnut Pastry (see opposite)

plain flour, for dusting

2 tablespoons olive oil

20g unsalted butter

1 onion, finely sliced

2 large leeks, sliced

150g Wensleydale cheese, coarsely grated

200ml double cream

100ml full-fat milk

3 large eggs plus 1 egg yolk

salt and black pepper

STEP 1

Heat the oven to 200°C/400°F/gas 6. Roll out the pastry on a lightly floured worktop to the thickness of a pound coin. Use to line a 30 x 20 x 3cm loose-bottomed fluted tart tin. Prick the base of the pastry case all over with a fork, then chill for at least 10 minutes.

STEP 2

Line the pastry case with baking paper and fill with baking beans or rice. Set the tin on a baking sheet. Place in the heated oven and bake blind for 15 minutes. Remove the paper and beans/rice, then bake for a further 5–10 minutes until golden. Remove from the oven. Turn the oven down to 160°C/325°F/gas 3.

STEP 3

While you are baking the pastry case, heat the oil and butter in a large frying pan and gently fry the onion and leeks for about 20 minutes until softened and golden. Season with salt and pepper. Spread the leek mixture in the tart case and scatter over the cheese.

STEP 4

In a jug, mix together the double cream, milk, eggs and egg yolk. Season with salt and pepper, then pour into the pastry case. Return to the oven and bake for 30–35 minutes until the filling is set but still has a slight wobble in the centre. Allow to cool for 15 minutes before serving.

WALNUT PASTRY

Ground nuts are a great addition to pastry, especially if you are baking a cheese-based quiche – they make it even more richly savoury. Nuts work well with sweet tarts, too. A little ground almond or hazelnut added to the pastry can take a chocolate or lemon tart from the realm of the ordinary and transform it into something magical. Be aware though that adding nuts will mean your pastry will darken more quickly during baking, so be careful not to let it burn.

MAKES ENOUGH TO LINE A 23CM ROUND DEEP TART TIN OR A 30 X 20 X 3CM RECTANGULAR TART TIN

YOU WILL NEED: A FOOD PROCESSOR

70g shelled walnuts

250g plain flour, plus extra for dusting

½ teaspoon salt

150g cold unsalted butter, cut into cubes

1 medium egg yolk

2–3 tablespoons cold water

STEP 1

Blitz the walnuts in a food processor until finely ground. Tip them into a mixing bowl and add the flour and salt. Add the butter and rub together with your fingertips until the mixture resembles breadcrumbs.

STEP 2

Add the egg yolk and mix in quickly with a flat-bladed knife, then mix in enough cold water, a little at a time, to bind the mixture into a dough.

STEP 3

Turn out onto a lightly floured worktop. Bring together and knead briefly until smooth, then shape into a disc. Wrap in clingfilm and chill for at least 15 minutes before using.

BEEF CHEEK, MUSHROOM AND MADEIRA PUFF PIE

For a good pie, the meat in the filling should be lusciously tender with a rich gravy and be topped with a golden layer of buttery pastry. It should definitely leave you wanting more. This pie delivers all that in spades. To get ahead, make the filling for the pie the day before you want to eat it so all you have to do is top it with pastry and bake. The day's rest will make the beef all the more tender.

SERVES 6

YOU WILL NEED: A LARGE PIE DISH
(ABOUT 1.5 LITRE); A PIE FUNNEL

vegetable oil, for frying

3 tablespoons plain flour, plus extra for dusting

1kg beef cheek, cut into 5cm pieces

200ml Madeira, plus an extra splash (about 45ml)

600ml hot beef stock

3 sprigs of fresh rosemary

30g butter

1 onion, finely chopped

2 garlic cloves, finely chopped

300g mixed mushrooms, such as halved button
   mushrooms and thickly sliced portobello and
   chestnut mushrooms

salt and black pepper

FOR THE PASTRY LIDS

1 x quantity Flaky Pastry (see page 157)

1 medium egg, beaten

STEP 1

Heat a thin layer of oil in a large flameproof casserole. Season the flour with salt and pepper, then use to coat the beef. Fry the beef, in batches, over a high heat until golden brown all over, adding more oil if necessary. As each batch is browned, remove with a slotted spoon to a plate. Set aside.

STEP 2

You should have lots of sticky golden bits on the base of your casserole (if they are burnt or taste bitter, deglaze the pot with water and discard the liquid). Add the 200ml Madeira and bubble away for a couple of minutes, scraping the tasty bits from the base of the pot, until reduced by half. Add the stock and return the beef to the casserole along with the rosemary. Bring to a simmer, then cover and cook for 2–2½ hours until the beef is really tender.

STEP 3

Meanwhile, melt the butter in a large frying pan over a medium-low heat and fry the onion for 5–10 minutes until softened but not coloured. Add the garlic and mushrooms, turn up the heat and fry until the mushrooms are turning golden and there is no moisture left in the pan. Stir in the extra Madeira and allow it to bubble away to about a tablespoon. Set aside.

Once the beef is cooked, remove it with a slotted spoon to a large pie dish (about 1.5 litre). Place a pie funnel in the centre of the dish. Return the casserole to the heat and bubble the sauce uncovered for 5–10 minutes until it has thickened and reduced by about a third. Pour the reduced sauce over the beef and add the mushroom mixture. Allow to cool.

STEP 5

Heat the oven to 200°C/400°F/gas 6. Roll out the pastry on a lightly floured worktop to the thickness of a pound coin. Brush the edge of the pie dish with beaten egg, then lay the pastry over the top and press around the edge to seal. Trim to fit and crimp the edge to make sure the pastry stays in place. Cut a small hole in the centre of the pastry lid so the pie funnel can peek through. If you like, decorate with the pastry trimmings cut into shapes. Brush all over with beaten egg.

STEP 6

Place the pie in the heated oven and bake for 35–40 minutes until golden brown. Serve hot, with seasonal vegetables.

FLAKY PASTRY

A quick flaky pastry gives you a buttery, light layered pastry, without all the rolling and folding that puff or rough puff pastry requires. It won't rise in quite the same way but will flake in the mouth with a lovely butteriness.

MAKES ENOUGH TO COVER A LARGE PIE

175g unsalted butter

225g plain flour

a good pinch of salt

2–3 tablespoons icy water

STEP 1

Wrap your piece of butter in foil and freeze for 45 minutes.

STEP 2

When you are ready to make the pastry, sift the flour and salt into a mixing bowl. Unwrap the frozen butter and, holding it with the foil so it doesn't slip from your grasp, coarsely grate it directly into the flour. Use a flat-bladed knife to stir the grated butter through the flour to coat all the butter strands.

STEP 3

Sprinkle with 2 tablespoons icy water. Use the knife to mix with a cutting motion until the mixture starts to come together to make a dough. You may need a tiny dash more water. Bring together with your hands and shape into a disc. Wrap the pastry in clingfilm and chill for 30 minutes before using.

CRAB AND ROASTED SPRING ONION TART

It's not often that a spring onion is treated like a cooking vegetable. Usually it is sliced and tossed through salads or used as a garnish. When roasted, spring onions become beautifully mellow, and matched with the sweet flavour of crab they make an unbeatable combination for a tart filling.

SERVES 6

YOU WILL NEED: A 20CM FLUTED TART TIN

200g spring onions, root end trimmed and
  a little taken from the green end

olive oil, for drizzling

375g all-butter puff pastry, thawed if frozen

plain flour, for dusting

2 medium eggs

150ml double cream

100ml crème fraîche

grated zest of 1 lemon

200g white crab meat

2 tablespoons very finely chopped fresh flat-leaf parsley

2 tablespoons brown crab meat

salt and black pepper

STEP 1

Heat the oven to 220°C/425°F/gas 7. Spread the spring onions in a small roasting tin. Add a good drizzle of olive oil and sprinkle with salt and pepper. Roast for 15 minutes, shaking the tin halfway through the time to turn the onions, until they are tender and starting to become golden. Remove and set aside. Reduce the oven temperature to 190°C/375°F/gas 5 and put a baking sheet in the oven to heat up.

STEP 2

Roll out the puff pastry on a lightly floured worktop and use to line a 20cm fluted tart tin.

STEP 3

In a jug, mix the eggs with the cream, crème fraîche, lemon zest and plenty of salt and pepper. Stir in the white crab meat and parsley.

STEP 4

Spread the brown crab meat evenly over the base of the tart case, then pour in the cream mixture. Arrange the spring onions over the top. Set the tin on the heated baking sheet in the oven and bake for about 25 minutes until the filling is set and golden (cover the filling with baking paper or foil if it is getting brown too quickly). Remove the tart from the oven and cool for 10–15 minutes before serving warm.

SPINACH AND GOAT'S CHEESE PUFF TART

Vegetarian

The wonderful combination of spinach and goat's cheese is shown off in this lovely tart, with the rich iron-like flavour of spinach being offset by the tangy creaminess of the goat's cheese. It may seem strange to line the tart case with puff pastry, but it really works – the buttery flakiness isn't lost by being filled. Setting the tart tin on a hot baking sheet in the oven will prevent the base of the pastry case getting soggy.

SERVES 4–6

YOU WILL NEED: A 23 X 15CM FLUTED LOOSE-BOTTOMED TART TIN

375g all-butter puff pastry, thawed if frozen

plain flour, for dusting

2 tablespoons olive oil

2 red onions, finely sliced

2 garlic cloves, crushed

500g baby leaf spinach

2 medium eggs plus 1 egg yolk

250ml crème fraîche

leaves picked from 2 sprigs of fresh oregano

150g goat's cheese log, crumbled

salt and black pepper

STEP 1

Heat the oven, with a baking sheet inside, to 200°C/400°F/gas 6. Roll out the puff pastry on a lightly floured worktop and use to line a 23 x 15cm fluted loose-bottomed tart tin. Prick the base all over with a fork, then chill in the fridge while you make the filling.

STEP 2

Heat the oil in a large frying pan and gently fry the onions over a medium heat for about 10 minutes until soft. Add the garlic and cook for a further minute. Spoon the onions and garlic onto a plate and spread out to cool.

STEP 3

Add the spinach to the frying pan and wilt over a low heat, then tip into a colander and run under cold water briefly to cool. Squeeze the spinach to remove as much excess liquid as possible. Add to the onions and garlic.

STEP 4

In a jug, beat the eggs and yolk with the crème fraîche and oregano leaves. Season well with salt and pepper.

STEP 5

Spread the spinach mixture in the chilled tart case, then sprinkle over the goat's cheese. Pour over the egg mixture. Set the tin on the heated baking sheet in the oven and bake for 25–30 minutes until the pastry is puffed and the filling set and golden. Leave to cool for 5 minutes before removing from the tin, and serve warm or at room temperature.

GRATIN DAUPHINOIS … BRAISED
RED CABBAGE … CELERIAC PURÉE
… CARAMELISED SHALLOTS …
CAULIFLOWER CHEESE … BRAISED
CHICORY IN WHITE WINE
… BROCCOLI WITH WALNUT
VINAIGRETTE … BALSAMIC AND
HAZELNUT BEETROOT … GINGER
CREAM PARSNIPS … BRAISED LEEKS
WITH A HERB CRUST

WINTER VEG

*It makes sense – in terms of flavour, freshness and cost –
to eat foods, particularly vegetables, in season, and there is
plenty on offer in the winter months.*

Cabbages are among the tastiest and most nutritious winter vegetables. Round, firm, red and white cabbages will sit happily in your fridge for weeks, waiting to be braised with spices or chestnuts and bacon. Savoy and January King are two of the most beautiful and delicious varieties at this time of year. And don't forget sprouts, which are just like dolly cabbages.

Although available all year round, cauliflower seems like a winter vegetable. Delicious eaten raw, dipped in garlicky mayo, when cooked the florets become mild in flavour, and seem to have been made to be smothered in a rich cheese sauce.

Celeriac is one of the weirdest-looking winter vegetables. Like its close cousin celery, it is delicious eaten raw, finely sliced and tossed into salads or coated in a mustardy mayo. But it's also superb mashed, enhanced with a sprinkling of nutmeg and a 'healthy' amount of double cream!

Winter is not without its share of salad-worthy leaves too. Crisp chicory (or endive) leaves, with their slightly bitter flavour, make a very refreshing salad with a simple dressing and a scattering of walnuts.

GRATIN DAUPHINOIS

Vegetarian

There are so many variations of this classic dish. Some use a waxy potato, while others add Parmesan or Gruyère cheese or finely sliced onion. This is the dish in its purest, most velvety form. If you wanted to serve it as a supper dish, you could add fried chunks of bacon, shredded ham hock or flaked smoked fish into the layers before baking.

SERVES 6

600ml double cream

1 garlic clove, cut in half

25g unsalted butter, softened

1kg floury potatoes, such as King Edward or Maris Piper, peeled

salt and black pepper

STEP 1

Heat the oven to 150°C/300°F/gas 2. Pour the cream into a saucepan and bring just to below boiling point, then set aside.

STEP 2

Rub the cut sides of the garlic halves all over the inside of a gratin dish or other shallow ovenproof dish, then butter the dish generously.

STEP 3

Finely slice the potatoes to about the thickness of a 20p coin – a mandolin is perfect for this, but you can also use a sharp knife. Layer up the potatoes in the gratin dish, seasoning each layer. Pour the cream evenly over the top.

STEP 4

Place in the heated oven and bake for 1 hour until tender, bubbling and golden brown. Serve hot.

BRAISED
RED CABBAGE

Vegetarian

With its tangy rich flavour and glossy dark red glow, it is easy to see why this dish is a winter staple, especially at Christmas time. The hours of long, gentle cooking temper and mellow the pungency of the vinegar and transform the once crunchy cabbage into lovely tender shreds.

SERVES 6–8

1 tablespoon olive or vegetable oil

50g butter

1 red onion, finely sliced

1 red cabbage, about 1kg, quartered, cored and finely shredded

2 star anise

1 cinnamon stick

3 tablespoons light soft brown sugar

2 fresh bay leaves

1 eating apple, peeled and coarsely grated

80ml red wine vinegar

100ml medium dry cider

salt and black pepper

STEP 1

Heat the oil and butter in a large, deep sauté pan. Add the onion and cook over a low heat for 10–12 minutes until soft.

STEP 2

Stir in the cabbage, spices, sugar, bay leaves, grated apple, vinegar and cider. Season well with salt and pepper. Bring to the boil, then reduce the heat to a simmer. Cover with a sheet of baking paper and then a lid. Braise gently for about 1½–2 hours, stirring occasionally. Taste and check the seasoning before serving hot.

CELERIAC PURÉE

Vegetarian

Celeriac manages to be both mild and packed with flavour at the same time. Cooking it in milk and then using the milk in the purée means that all that wonderful taste is locked in, rather than being thrown away with the cooking water. Celeriac purée is wonderfully creamy and velvety and never goes sticky like potatoes sometimes do, but to ensure the smoothest of purées it is best to use a hand blender if you have one.

SERVES 6

YOU WILL NEED: A HAND BLENDER

200g floury potatoes, peeled and cut into medium-sized chunks

1 large celeriac, weighing about 700g, peeled and cut into medium-sized chunks

570ml full-fat milk

30g butter

a small handful of fresh flat-leaf parsley, finely chopped

freshly grated nutmeg

salt and black pepper

STEP 1

Put the potatoes in a saucepan of cold salted water. Put the celeriac in another pan and pour in the milk. Bring both to the boil, then simmer gently for about 15 minutes until the potatoes and celeriac are tender.

STEP 2

Drain the potatoes and celeriac, reserving the milk from the celeriac. Put the potatoes and celeriac in the celeriac pan and use a hand blender to blend to a smooth purée, adding as much of the reserved milk as you need. Stir in the butter and parsley and season with nutmeg, salt and pepper. Serve hot.

ROASTED CARAMELISED SHALLOTS

Vegetarian

Smaller and milder than large onions, shallots are incredibly delicious roasted. These sticky little globes could almost make a meal on their own, served with buttery mash or cheesy polenta, but are equally happy sitting on the plate alongside most roasts you can think of.

SERVES 6

800g shallots

50g unsalted butter

1 tablespoon olive oil

45g caster sugar

50ml red wine vinegar

5–6 sprigs of fresh thyme

salt and black pepper

STEP 1

Heat the oven to 200°C/400°F/gas 6. Put the shallots into a bowl and cover with boiling water. Leave for 5 minutes, then drain and peel.

STEP 2

Heat the butter and oil in an ovenproof frying pan or small, heavy roasting tin. When the fat is foaming, add the shallots and sprinkle over the sugar. Cook, tossing, until the shallots start to colour and become sticky.

STEP 3

Add the vinegar, thyme and plenty of salt and pepper. Transfer to the heated oven and roast the shallots, tossing occasionally, for 30–40 minutes until golden brown and slightly sticky. Serve hot.

CAULIFLOWER CHEESE

Vegetarian

Cauli cheese – tender little tree-like florets smothered in a rich cheese sauce – is one of the all-time great vegetable dishes. Although not strictly traditional, a crunchy golden topping of crumbs and extra cheese sets the whole thing off perfectly. It makes a simple supper just as it is, but you could also try adding some blue cheese to the sauce, or fried bacon lardons.

SERVES 6

750ml full-fat milk

1 small onion, halved and studded with 2 cloves

1 fresh bay leaf

4 black peppercorns

50g butter

50g plain flour

100ml double cream

150g mature Cheddar cheese, grated

1 large cauliflower, broken into equal-size florets

100g fresh white breadcrumbs

salt and black pepper

STEP 1
Heat the milk in a saucepan with the clove-studded onion halves, bay leaf and peppercorns. When it starts to steam, remove from the heat and set aside to infuse for 10–15 minutes. Strain the milk into a jug.

STEP 2
Heat the grill to medium. Melt the butter in the saucepan. Add the flour and stir for a minute, then gradually add the milk, stirring, to make a smooth sauce. Bubble for 2 minutes, then remove from the heat. Stir in the cream and 125g of the Cheddar. Season well with salt and pepper.

STEP 3
While the sauce is bubbling, cook the cauliflower in a pan of boiling salted water for about 4 minutes until just tender. Drain well and tip into a flameproof serving dish.

STEP 4
Pour the hot cheese sauce over the cauliflower and mix together gently. Mix the remaining cheese with the breadcrumbs and scatter evenly over the top. Place under the heated grill and grill until golden and bubbling. Serve hot.

BRAISED CHICORY IN WHITE WINE AND PARSLEY

The pleasantly bitter notes of chicory are mellowed by braising it with honey and wine. This dish makes a particularly good partner for roast pork — the flavours complement the rich meat perfectly.

SERVES 6–8

4 large or 6 small chicory, halved lengthways
(or quartered if large)

60g butter, in small pieces

1 tablespoon runny honey, or to taste

75ml dry white wine

125ml hot vegetable stock

2 tablespoons finely chopped fresh flat-leaf parsley

salt and black pepper

STEP 1

Heat the oven to 180°C/350°F/gas 4. Put the chicory halves, cut-side up, in an ovenproof dish. Dot all over with the butter and drizzle over the honey. Pour in the wine and stock.

STEP 2

Season with black pepper and a little salt, then cover the dish with foil. Place in the heated oven and braise for 20–25 minutes, then remove the foil and cook for a further 10 minutes until the chicory is really tender. Sprinkle with the parsley and serve hot.

BROCCOLI WITH WALNUT VINAIGRETTE AND CRISPY SHALLOTS

Vegetarian

A sharp and nutty vinaigrette soaks into spears of just-cooked broccoli, giving it bags of flavour. To turn this into a simple supper, toss the dressed broccoli through cooked pasta and top with shavings of Parmesan.

SERVES 6

vegetable oil, for frying

2 banana shallots OR 4 small shallots, finely sliced

flaky sea salt

3 tablespoons lemon juice

a good pinch of sugar

1 garlic clove, crushed

4 tablespoons extra-virgin olive oil

2 tablespoons walnut oil

600g broccoli, trimmed

salt and black pepper

STEP 1
Heat a good layer (about 1cm deep) of vegetable oil in a frying pan over a low heat and fry the shallots for 10–12 minutes until they are deep golden and crisp. Drain on kitchen paper, then sprinkle with sea salt and set aside.

STEP 2
Whisk the lemon juice with the sugar, garlic and plenty of salt and pepper. Whisk in the extra-virgin olive oil and the walnut oil.

STEP 3
Plunge the broccoli into a pan of boiling water and cook for 3–4 minutes until just tender. Drain well. Pour the vinaigrette over the hot broccoli and toss to combine.

STEP 4
Scatter the crispy shallots over the broccoli just before serving so that they stay crisp.

ROASTED BALSAMIC AND HAZELNUT BEETROOT

Vegetarian

A fantastic side dish, this would sit just as well with pan-fried or whole roasted fish as it would a roasted joint. For a really easy supper dish, cut the roasted beetroot into smaller chunks and toss it through cooked couscous with lots of lemon and chopped parsley plus some crumbled feta.

SERVES 6

750g raw beetroots, peeled and cut into wedges

1 bulb of garlic, cloves separated but unpeeled

leaves picked from 1 sprig of fresh rosemary

olive oil, for drizzling

2–3 tablespoons aged balsamic vinegar

75g blanched (peeled) hazelnuts

salt and black pepper

STEP 1
Heat the oven to 190°C/375°F/gas 5. Place the beetroot wedges in a roasting tin with the garlic cloves and rosemary leaves. Drizzle generously with olive oil. Place in the heated oven and roast for 20 minutes.

STEP 2
Remove from the oven and add the balsamic vinegar and plenty of salt and pepper. Toss the beetroot wedges to coat with the oil and vinegar. Return to the oven and roast for a further 20–25 minutes until tender.

STEP 3
Meanwhile, toast the hazelnuts in a dry frying pan over a medium-low heat, tossing regularly, for a couple of minutes until starting to turn golden. Tip into a bowl to cool, then roughly chop. Scatter the nuts over the roasted beetroots before serving.

GINGER CREAM
PARSNIPS

Vegetarian

It can be very easy to get fed up with root vegetables in the middle of winter. But rather than buying out of season veg from far-flung places, try to be a bit more creative with our home-grown produce. These parsnips in a gingery cream are fabulous alongside a roast chicken or roast beef, but you could also use them as the base of a vegetarian pie – cook some batons of celeriac with the parsnips, then stir in some wilted spinach or chard, spoon into a pie dish and top with flaky or shortcrust pastry before baking to a golden finish.

SERVES 6–8

800g parsnips, peeled and cut into batons
  (little finger thickness)

2 tablespoons olive oil

1 banana shallot OR 2 small shallots, finely sliced

2 garlic cloves, finely sliced

2 tablespoons finely grated fresh root ginger

1 sprig of fresh rosemary

2 teaspoons ground ginger

400ml double cream

salt and black pepper

STEP 1

Par-boil the parsnips in a pan of boiling water for 3–4 minutes. Drain in a colander and leave to steam dry, covered with a tea towel, for a minute or two.

STEP 2

Heat the oil in a large frying pan over a medium-low heat and gently fry the shallot for about 10 minutes until soft but not browned. Add the garlic, fresh ginger and rosemary and cook for a further minute.

STEP 3

Add the parsnips to the pan and toss well to coat with the flavoured oil, then add the ground ginger, cream and plenty of salt and pepper. Simmer for 6–8 minutes until the parsnips are tender and the cream is thickened. Serve hot.

BRAISED LEEKS WITH A HERB AND PARMESAN CRUST

Vegetarian

This easy side dish can be left to simmer in the oven, becoming tender and succulent, while you get on with making your main dish. You can use whatever cheese you like in the crust — for example, try a nutty Gruyère or tangy Cheddar instead of Parmesan.

SERVES 6

3 large leeks

100ml vegetable stock

3 tablespoons double cream

a large handful of fresh breadcrumbs

2 tablespoons finely chopped fresh parsley

1 tablespoon picked fresh thyme leaves

40g Parmesan cheese, freshly grated

salt and black pepper

STEP 1

Heat the oven to 190°C/375°F/gas 5. Cut each leek across into 3 pieces, then halve each piece lengthways. Arrange the leeks in an ovenproof dish and pour over the stock and cream. Season well with salt and pepper. Cover with foil, then place in the heated oven and braise for 15 minutes.

STEP 2

Mix together the breadcrumbs, herbs and Parmesan. Uncover the dish and sprinkle the crumb mixture evenly over the leeks. Return to the oven and bake, uncovered, for 25–30 minutes until the leeks are tender and the crumb topping is golden brown. Serve hot.

TREACLE TART ... SWEET
SHORTCRUST PASTRY ... TARTE TATIN
... APPLE AND CUSTARD CRUMBLE ...
CHOCOLATE AND HAZELNUT
TORTE ... ORANGE AND PASSION
FRUIT TART ... STICKY TOFFEE
PUDDINGS ... HOT CHOCOLATE
SPONGE WITH CHOCOLATE SAUCE
... RHUBARB COBBLER ... AUTUMN
FRUIT STRUDEL ... ORANGE-SPIKED
BREAD AND BUTTER PUDDING ...
BAKED BOOZY APPLES ... APPLE AND
QUINCE PIE ... TREACLE
AND LEMON SPONGE

PUDDINGS

After the colourful riot of summer fruits, with their brash aromas and flavours, the fruits of autumn and winter may seem dull, but they are just as wonderful in their own subtle way and perfect for making cold-weather puddings.

Delicious varieties of apple ripen now, and gluts will keep all winter long, becoming sweeter with the passing weeks. Depending on the variety you use, you can change the way your puddings taste and their texture. Some apples will break down into a purée, much like a Bramley apple but with less acidity, and others will stay resolutely firm during cooking.

Like apples, the quince is part of the rose family, which explains its distinctive rose-like scent. Combined with apples and baked under a sweet pastry crust, it makes a delectable pie. Bright pink forced rhubarb is another mouth-puckeringly tart fruit that melts to a silky smoothness when cooked. Used in a cobbler filling, rhubarb brings a welcome splash of colour to the winter table.

TREACLE TART

You may have wondered why puddings such as treacle tart and treacle sponge are so-called when they are made with golden syrup. In fact, the word 'treacle' refers to any syrup that is produced in the process of refining sugar, from the light and sweet golden syrup through to the darkest syrup of all, molasses. With a dollop of whisky cream (see Note), treacle tart makes an indulgent pudding for entertaining, but you could also eat it in thin slices on its own with a cuppa, as a sort of posh flapjack.

SERVES 8–10

YOU WILL NEED: A 23CM FLUTED TART TIN

1 x quantity Sweet Shortcrust Pastry (see page 182)

plain flour, for dusting

750g golden syrup

½ teaspoon ground ginger

125g fine fresh breadcrumbs

30g rolled oats

2 large eggs, lightly beaten

finely grated zest of 1 large lemon

STEP 1

Roll out the pastry on a lightly floured worktop to the thickness of a 20p coin. Use to line a 23cm fluted tart tin. Prick the base all over with a fork, then chill in the fridge for 30 minutes.

STEP 2

Heat the oven, with a baking sheet inside, to 200°C/400°F/gas 6. Line the pastry case with baking paper and fill with baking beans or rice. Set the tin on the hot baking sheet in the oven and bake blind for 12 minutes. Remove the paper and beans/rice, then return to the oven to bake for about 5 minutes until the pastry case is golden. Remove and set aside. Reduce the oven temperature to 180°C/350°F/gas 4.

STEP 3

For the filling, put the golden syrup in a saucepan, add the ginger and gently warm until quite liquid. Remove from the heat. Stir in the breadcrumbs, rolled oats, eggs and lemon zest, mixing well. Pour into the pastry case.

STEP 4

Place in the oven and bake for 30–35 minutes until the filling is golden and just set. Remove from the oven and leave to cool for at least 15 minutes before serving, or cool completely.

NOTE

To make a whisky cream to serve with the tart, lightly whip 300ml double cream with 1–2 tablespoons whisky and 2 tablespoons icing sugar until thick, then fold in the finely grated zest of ½ lemon and a squeeze of juice.

SWEET SHORTCRUST PASTRY

This is a simple variation on the Enriched Shortcrust Pastry used in the Pies and Tarts chapter (page 145), which has a little caster sugar added in for extra sweetness.

MAKES ENOUGH TO LINE A 23CM DEEP TART TIN

250g plain flour, plus extra for dusting

½ teaspoon salt

160g cold unsalted butter, diced

75g golden caster sugar

1 medium egg yolk

1–2 tablespoons cold water

STEP 1

Sift the flour and salt into a mixing bowl. Rub in the butter with your fingertips until you have a crumble-like mixture, then stir in the caster sugar until completely mixed in.

STEP 2

Add the egg yolk and mix in quickly with a flat-bladed knife, then mix in enough cold water, a little at a time, to bind the mixture into a dough.

STEP 3

Turn out onto a lightly floured worktop. Bring together and knead briefly until smooth, then shape into a disc. Wrap in clingfilm and chill for at least 15 minutes before using.

SPICED TARTE TATIN

When making a Tarte Tatin the best advice is not to panic. Yes, caramel can have its stroppy moments, but as long as you don't stir once the sugar has melted — just swirl it in the pan — and let it bubble until it is thick and a rich mahogany colour, all will be well.

SERVES 8

YOU WILL NEED: A HEAVY-BASED 20CM OVENPROOF FRYING PAN

6–8 crunchy eating apples, such as Braeburn

200g caster sugar

4 tablespoons water

60g unsalted butter, cut into cubes

2 star anise

1 generous teaspoon vanilla bean paste

6 black peppercorns

375g all-butter puff pastry, thawed if frozen

plain flour, for dusting

STEP 1

Peel and halve the apples, then scoop out the cores; set the apples aside. Put the sugar in a heavy-based 20cm ovenproof frying pan (measure across the base) with the water and gently dissolve the sugar over a low heat. Turn up the heat and boil, without stirring, for 5–10 minutes to make a caramel a few shades darker than golden syrup. The caramel needs to be dark enough so it isn't too sweet but not too dark or it will be bitter.

STEP 2

Immediately remove from the heat and stir in the butter — the mixture will foam quite vigorously. Keep stirring until smooth. Add the star anise, vanilla bean paste and peppercorns.

STEP 3

Arrange the apple halves, cut-side up, in the caramel so they fill the pan — you can squish them in together quite closely as they will shrink a little when they are cooked. Set the pan back over a gentle heat and cook for about 5 minutes until the bottoms of the apple halves take on some colour. The caramel should start bubbling around the apples. Remove from the heat and leave to cool completely

STEP 4

Heat the oven to 220°C/425°F/gas 7. Roll out the pastry on a lightly floured worktop to the thickness of a pound coin. Lay the pastry over the apples in the pan. Trim off excess pastry around the rim of the pan, then carefully tuck the pastry edge down inside the pan, around the apples.

STEP 5

Place the pan in the heated oven and bake for 25–30 minutes until the pastry is dark golden and puffed. Remove from the oven and leave to settle for 5 minutes, then carefully invert the tart on to a serving plate. Serve with cream or ice cream.

APPLE AND CUSTARD CRUMBLE

Everyone loves a good crumble with lashings of thick custard, so why not combine the two? Having the custard inside the crumble adds a completely new dimension – tender chunks of tart apple encased in a rich custard blanket with a crumbly topping.

SERVES 8

YOU WILL NEED: A 1.2 LITRE OVENPROOF DISH

175ml full-fat milk

150ml double cream

2 large egg yolks

2 teaspoons cornflour

50g golden caster sugar

freshly grated nutmeg

4 cloves

3 large Bramley apples, peeled, cored and cut into wedges

a squeeze of lemon juice

50g light soft brown sugar

FOR THE CRUMBLE

250g plain flour

200g cold unsalted butter, diced

30g demerara sugar

30g golden caster sugar

1 teaspoon ground cinnamon

1 teaspoon ground ginger

finely grated zest of 1 lemon

STEP 1

First make the crumble. Put the flour in a large mixing bowl and rub in the butter with your fingertips to make a coarse crumbly mixture. Stir in both the sugars, the spices and lemon zest.

STEP 2

Heat the milk and cream in a saucepan until almost boiling. Meanwhile, whisk the egg yolks with the cornflour and caster sugar in a heatproof bowl. Pour the hot creamy milk over the egg yolks and whisk together. Return to the washed-out pan and cook over a low heat, stirring constantly, until the custard is thick enough to coat the back of the spoon. Stir in a good grating of nutmeg and the cloves, then pour into a jug.

STEP 3

Heat the oven to 180°C/350°F/gas 4. Mix together the apples, lemon juice and brown sugar and tumble into a 1.2 litre ovenproof dish. Pour the custard over the apples and give the dish a wiggle to make sure the custard settles to the bottom. Scatter the crumble mixture evenly over the top. Place in the heated oven and bake for about 50 minutes until the crumble is golden brown and the custard has set. Serve hot.

CHOCOLATE AND HAZELNUT TORTE

A subtle hint of booze and a crunch of hazelnut go so well with chocolate in this luscious rich torte. A real showstopper, it will wow your friends and family, and all the while you can keep your secret – that it involves very little work from the cook!

SERVES 16

YOU WILL NEED: 1 X 20CM WATERTIGHT CAKE TIN

250g unsalted butter, plus extra for greasing

cocoa powder, for dusting

250g dark chocolate (70% cocoa solids), roughly chopped

250g caster sugar

85ml Frangelico liqueur

4 tablespoons plain flour

50g toasted hazelnuts, finely chopped

4 large eggs

STEP 1

Heat the oven to 130°C/250°F/gas 1. Butter a 20 cm watertight cake tin and dust with cocoa powder. Line the bottom with a circle of baking paper.

STEP 2

Melt the butter, chocolate and sugar together in a heavy-based saucepan over a very gentle heat, stirring until smooth. Add the Frangelico and remove from the heat. Stir in the flour, hazelnuts and eggs, then whisk until smoothly combined. Pour into the prepared tin.

STEP 3

Set the cake tin in a roasting tin and pour enough boiling water into the roasting tin to half fill it. Place in the heated oven and bake for 1–1¼ hours until the centre of the torte is set and springy to the touch.

STEP 4

Remove from the tin of water and leave to cool in the cake tin for 30 minutes before turning out onto a serving plate. Chill in the fridge for 3–4 hours or overnight. About half an hour before serving, remove from the fridge to bring up to room temperature. Finish the torte with a dusting of cocoa powder.

BLOOD ORANGE AND PASSION FRUIT TART

This tart is a lovely way to use blood oranges, which are around for such a short time.

SERVES 8–10

YOU WILL NEED: A 25CM-ROUND, 3CM-DEEP FLUTED TART TIN

250g plain flour, plus extra for dusting

25g icing sugar, sifted

150g cold unsalted butter, cut into pieces

2 medium egg yolks

about 1 tablespoon cold water

1 medium egg white, beaten to mix

FOR THE FILLING

grated zest and juice of 1 large lemon

125ml blood orange (sanguinello) juice

3 wrinkled passion fruit

6 medium eggs

250g caster sugar

150ml double cream

STEP 1
Put the flour and icing sugar in a bowl. Add the butter, rubbing it into the dry ingredients with your fingertips until the mixture resembles fine breadcrumbs. Add the egg yolks and cold water and mix until a soft dough forms. Gently knead the dough to form a disc, wrap in clingfilm and chill for 30 minutes. Roll out the pastry on a floured worktop to just under pound-coin thickness; use to line the tart tin. Trim any excess pastry and prick the base all over with a fork. Chill for 30 minutes.

STEP 2
Heat the oven to 200°C/400°F/gas 6, with a baking sheet inside. Line the tart case with baking paper and fill with baking beans or rice. Set the tin on the hot baking sheet and bake for 12–15 minutes until the edges of the pastry are set and start to colour. Remove the paper and beans/rice, then return to the oven to bake for 2–3 minutes or until the pastry is a light golden colour. Brush the inside of the case with beaten egg white, then bake for another 2 minutes. Set aside to cool. Turn the oven down to 120°C/230°F/gas ¼.

STEP 3
Combine the lemon and orange juices in a bowl. Cut the passion fruit in half and scoop out the flesh into a sieve set over the bowl. Press the flesh in the sieve, releasing the juice; discard the seeds. You should now have 150–175ml of juices.

STEP 4
Gently whisk together the eggs and sugar. Add the juices and cream, then pass through a sieve into a clean bowl. Stir in the lemon zest. Place the pastry case, still on the baking sheet, in the oven. Pour the filling into the case, then carefully slide the sheet into the oven. Bake for 45–50 minutes until the filling is just set with a slight wobble. Leave to cool.

STICKY TOFFEE PUDDINGS

Sticky toffee pudding has won a place in our hearts as one of the all-time great winter puddings. There is something magical about its light sponge drenched with creamy toffee sauce. If you want to make one big pudding instead of individual puddings, pour the batter into a large (2.5 litre) ovenproof dish and bake for 30–35 minutes.

MAKES 8 PUDDINGS

YOU WILL NEED: 8 X 100ML INDIVIDUAL PUDDING MOULDS; A HAND-HELD ELECTRIC MIXER

75g unsalted butter, softened, plus extra for greasing

200g Medjool dates, pitted and finely chopped

250ml hot water

1 teaspoon bicarbonate of soda

50g golden caster sugar

100g dark muscovado sugar

2 medium eggs, lightly beaten

180g self-raising flour

1 teaspoon each baking powder and ground ginger

FOR THE TOFFEE SAUCE

125g unsalted butter

80g dark muscovado sugar

50g golden caster sugar

1 teaspoon vanilla extract

250ml double cream

2 tablespoons dark rum

STEP 1
Heat the oven to 180°C/350°F/gas 4. Grease 8 individual 100ml pudding moulds with softened butter and set aside. Put the dates in a bowl, cover with the hot water and sprinkle in the bicarbonate of soda. Set aside for 10 minutes.

STEP 2
Using an electric mixer, beat the butter with the 2 sugars until light and fluffy. Gradually beat in the eggs. Sift the flour, baking powder and ground ginger over the egg mixture and fold in, then mix in the soaked dates with their water. The mixture will be very wet but don't worry. Divide it among the pudding moulds and set them on a baking sheet. Place in the heated oven and bake for 15–20 minutes until a skewer inserted into each pudding comes out clean.

STEP 3
Make the sauce while the puddings are baking. Put the butter, 2 sugars, vanilla and cream in a saucepan and warm over a medium heat until the butter has melted and the sugar dissolved. Bring to the boil and cook for 3 minutes. Stir in the rum and cook for a further 1–2 minutes.

STEP 4
Turn out the puddings and serve with the hot sauce drizzled over the top.

HOT CHOCOLATE SPONGE WITH CHOCOLATE SAUCE

This luscious pudding brings back memories of the best of school puds. The sauce here is a more grown-up affair, but if you want the authentic taste of childhood you could simply add some cocoa powder to a vanilla custard.

SERVES 8

YOU WILL NEED: A 20CM SQUARE CAKE OR BROWNIE TIN; A HAND-HELD ELECTRIC MIXER

250g unsalted butter, softened, plus extra for greasing

100g dark chocolate (70% cocoa solids), broken up

4 medium eggs, beaten

150g golden caster sugar

100g dark soft brown sugar

250g self-raising flour

1 teaspoon baking powder

1 teaspoon vanilla extract

125ml full-fat milk, warmed

FOR THE CHOCOLATE SAUCE

200ml full-fat milk

400ml double cream

100g dark chocolate (70% cocoa solids), broken up

2 tablespoons golden syrup

2 tablespoons dark rum (optional)

STEP 1
Heat the oven to 180°C/350°F/gas 4. Grease a square 20cm cake or brownie tin with soft butter, then line the base with baking paper.

STEP 2
Put the butter and chocolate into a heatproof bowl and set over a pan of barely simmering water (don't let the base of the bowl touch the water). Leave to melt, without stirring, then remove from the heat and stir until smooth.

STEP 3
Using an electric mixer, whisk the eggs with the 2 sugars for 3–4 minutes until pale and fluffy. Fold in the chocolate mixture followed by the flour, baking powder and vanilla extract. Add enough warm milk to make a thickish mixture that will drop off the spoon when it is gently shaken.

STEP 4
Pour the mixture into the tin and spread evenly. Place in the heated oven and bake for 45–50 minutes until a skewer inserted into the centre of the sponge comes out clean. Remove from the oven and leave to settle while you make the sauce.

STEP 5
Heat the milk and cream in a pan until almost boiling. Put the chocolate and syrup in a bowl. Pour the hot milk over the chocolate to melt it, then stir until smooth. Add the rum, if using. Cut the sponge into squares and serve with the hot chocolate sauce drizzled over the top.

RHUBARB COBBLER

A rustic-looking cobbler is irresistible – it demands that you dig in, lifting the cobbles to find what's underneath. Here it is bright pink rhubarb, which adds a splash of colour to winter puds. A cobbler was most likely first created in the British colonies. Unable to make traditional suet puddings, the colonists layered up fruits (or meats) topped with a scone dough before baking.

SERVES 6

YOU WILL NEED: A 2 LITRE OVENPROOF DISH

900g forced rhubarb, cut into 3cm pieces

175g golden caster sugar

finely grated zest and juice of 1 orange

1 vanilla pod, split open

1 teaspoon cornflour

250g self-raising flour

1 teaspoon baking powder

½ teaspoon salt

50g ground almonds

100g cold unsalted butter, cut into chunks

190ml buttermilk

1 large egg

demerera sugar, for sprinkling

STEP 1
Heat the oven to 200°C/400°F/gas 6. Put the rhubarb, 125g of the sugar and the orange zest into a 2 litre ovenproof dish. Scrape the seeds from the vanilla pod into the dish and add the pod too. Mix the orange juice with the cornflour and pour into the dish. Stir to mix everything together. Cover the dish with foil, then place in the heated oven and bake for about 10 minutes while you make the topping.

STEP 2
Sift the flour, baking powder and salt into a bowl. Add the ground almonds, remaining 50g of caster sugar and butter and rub into the flour mixture with your fingertips until it forms pea-sized crumbs. In a jug, whisk the buttermilk with the egg, then pour this into the flour mixture and stir until it just comes together.

STEP 3
Remove the dish from the oven and take off the foil. Divide the dough into 12–14 equal pieces and roll each into a rough ball. Dot them all over the surface of the rhubarb.

STEP 4
Return the dish to the oven, uncovered, and bake for 30–40 minutes until the cobbler topping is golden brown and the rhubarb juices are bubbling around the edges. Sprinkle with demerara sugar and serve hot, with pouring cream.

AUTUMN FRUIT STRUDEL

True strudel pastry is extraordinarily tricky to make, involving much patience. Filo is the usual substitute for strudel pastry, but butter puff pastry, rolled really thin, works well too. Strudel freezes well so you could double the quantity of filling and make a second strudel to freeze (uncooked) for another time (bake from frozen, adding an extra 10 minutes to the baking time).

SERVES 6

YOU WILL NEED: 1 BAKING SHEET, LINED WITH BAKING PAPER

1 x 375g ready-rolled sheet of butter puff pastry, thawed if frozen

plain flour, for dusting

15g unsalted butter, melted

3 tablespoons blackberry jam or jelly

4 tablespoons ground almonds

1 small Bramley apple

1 firm Conference or Comice pear

a handful of ripe blackberries (about 70g)

½ teaspoon ground allspice

1 tablespoon caster sugar or light brown muscovado sugar

1 egg, beaten

icing sugar, for dusting

STEP 1

Heat the oven to 190°C/375°F/gas 5. Cut the sheet of pastry widthways in half. You are only going to use one half of the sheet, so wrap the rest and use another time, or double the filling ingredients and make 2 strudels (see introduction).

STEP 2

Roll out the half pastry sheet on a lightly floured surface to make a 30 x 40cm rectangle (the pastry will get very thin). Lightly brush the melted butter over the pastry, leaving a 2.5cm border clear. Spread the jam or jelly on the butter, within the border, and scatter the ground almonds evenly over the top.

STEP 3

Peel and core the apple. Grate into a colander, then squeeze out as much juice as you can. Peel, core and finely slice the pear. Mix with the apple and the blackberries. Spread the fruit evenly over the pastry (within the border), then sprinkle with the allspice and caster or brown sugar.

STEP 4

Starting on one long side, carefully roll up the pastry to form a log shape. Turn it over so the seal is underneath, then tuck the ends under. Brush all over with beaten egg. Transfer to the lined baking sheet.

STEP 5

Place in the heated oven and bake for about 30 minutes until golden and puffed up. Transfer to a wire rack and leave to cool a little before dusting with icing sugar and serving with lots of double cream or custard.

ORANGE-SPIKED BREAD AND BUTTER PUDDING

Orange lends a subtle floral note that spikes through the sweet softness of this bread and butter pudding. The lovely open crumb of brioche readily absorbs the custard but you could use any bread you have, or try leftover panettone. If you like your custard particularly silky, you can set the pudding dish in a roasting tin half-filled with boiling water.

SERVES 6–8

YOU WILL NEED: A LARGE OVENPROOF DISH (ABOUT 1.5 LITRE)

125g plump raisins

75ml brandy

2 teaspoons orange flower water

125g unsalted butter, softened, plus extra for greasing

12 slices slightly stale brioche loaf

300ml full-fat milk

400ml double cream

1 teaspoon vanilla extract

freshly grated nutmeg

2 medium eggs plus 3 egg yolks

75g golden caster sugar

grated zest of 2 oranges

demerara sugar, for sprinkling

STEP 1
Put the raisins and brandy in a small pan over a low heat and warm gently. Remove from the heat and stir in the orange flower water. Set aside for 15 minutes so the raisins can absorb the liquid.

STEP 2
Butter one side of each brioche slice, then cut them in half to make triangles. Layer the brioche triangles, butter-side up, in a large ovenproof dish (about 1.5 litre), scattering the raisins and their liquid in between the layers. Make sure the triangles overlap a little so they stick up.

STEP 3
Put the milk, cream, vanilla and a good grating of nutmeg in a saucepan. Bring to just below boiling point. Meanwhile, whisk together the eggs, egg yolks, caster sugar and orange zest in a large heatproof bowl. Pour the hot creamy milk into the egg mixture and whisk well to combine. Pour this custard evenly over the brioche and press the triangles down lightly, making sure the custard gets into all the gaps. Set aside for 20 minutes so the brioche can absorb the custard.

STEP 4
Heat the oven to 180°C/350°F/gas 4. Sprinkle a little demerara sugar over the surface of the pudding. Place in the heated oven and bake for 30–35 minutes until the custard is just set and the pudding is golden brown. If it starts to become too brown during cooking, cover loosely with foil. Leave the pudding to stand for 10–15 minutes before serving in generous scoops.

BAKED BOOZY APPLES

Baked apples are like an old friend, always there when we need comfort. If you hollow out a little more in the centre of your apple, you can pack in the maximum boozy fruitiness.

SERVES 6

YOU WILL NEED: AN APPLE CORER

75g unsalted butter, softened

50g light muscovado sugar

4 tablespoons Calvados or brandy

100g mixed sultanas and raisins

½ teaspoon ground allspice

freshly grated nutmeg

finely grated zest of 1 lemon

6 eating apples

toasted flaked almonds, to finish

STEP 1

Put the butter, sugar and Calvados or brandy in a small pan and heat gently until the butter melts and the sugar dissolves. Remove from the heat and add the dried fruit, spices and lemon zest. Stir to mix, then leave to cool – the fruit will absorb the liquid and the butter will solidify around them.

STEP 2

Heat the oven to 180°C/350°F/gas 4. Using an apple corer, cut the cores out of the whole apples. Make the opening a little bigger by coring again, slightly off-centre. Score each apple horizontally around its middle so it won't burst during baking.

STEP 3

Arrange the apples in a baking dish and fill the hollows with the buttery fruit. Add a little splash of water to the dish around the apples. Place in the heated oven and bake for about 30 minutes until the apples are soft and tender. Scatter toasted flaked almonds over the apples and serve with custard or ice cream.

APPLE AND QUINCE PIE

The quince is an unusual fruit. It will survive even the harshest winters, and it will happily sit in your fruit bowl for weeks waiting to be used. Tough as anything and a real labour of love to peel and core, they become soft and delicate once cooked, with a texture as smooth as silk and a perfumed fragrance that is like the mingling of rose and honey.

SERVES 6

YOU WILL NEED: A 23CM PIE DISH

1 lemon, cut in half

600g Bramley apples

1 quince, about 200g

2 tablespoons caster sugar, plus extra for sprinkling

2 tablespoons light soft brown sugar

20g cold unsalted butter, cut into small cubes

plain flour, for dusting

1 x quantity Sweet Shortcrust Pastry (see page 182) or Shortcrust Pastry for Mince Pies (see page 145)

1 medium egg, lightly beaten

STEP 1

Heat the oven to 220°C/425°F/gas 7. Squeeze the juice from half of the lemon into a bowl of cold water. Peel and core the apples, then cut into chunks. As each apple is cut, put the chunks into the lemon water to stop them browning. Peel and core the quince. Cut two-thirds of the quince into chunks and add to the bowl of lemon water; grate the final third of quince and add to the bowl.

STEP 2

Drain the fruit and tip into a 23cm pie dish. Add the juice from the other lemon half and both the sugars. Stir to mix with the fruit, then dot the butter all over the top. Put a pie funnel in the centre of the fruit, if you have one.

STEP 3

Roll out the pastry on a lightly floured surface to the thickness of a pound coin. Dampen the rim of the pie dish, then lay the pastry over the dish and press to the rim to seal. Trim off excess pastry and crimp the pastry edge with your fingers. Decorate the lid with any pastry trimmings cut into pretty shapes, stuck on with beaten egg. Brush the pastry lid with beaten egg and sprinkle with caster sugar. Cut a steam hole in the centre, directly over the pie funnel if you have used one.

STEP 4

Place in the heated oven and bake for 15 minutes. Turn the oven down to 190°C/375°F/gas 5 and bake for a further 30–35 minutes until golden brown. Remove from the oven and leave to settle for 10 minutes or so before serving with cream.

TREACLE AND LEMON SPONGE

Just thinking about plunging your spoon into a warm treacle sponge trickled with cream is enough to banish even the most severe case of winter blues. It's so easy to make – a simple cake mixture is transformed by the power of steam into a rib-stickingly good dessert.

SERVES 6

YOU WILL NEED: A 1 LITRE PUDDING BASIN; A HAND-HELD ELECTRIC MIXER

150g unsalted butter, softened, plus extra for greasing

5 tablespoons golden syrup

150g golden caster sugar

finely grated zest of 1 lemon

2 large eggs

1 teaspoon vanilla extract

150g self-raising flour

about 75ml milk

STEP 1

Grease a 1 litre pudding basin with softened butter. Spoon the golden syrup into the base.

STEP 2

Using an electric mixer, beat the butter with the sugar and lemon zest for about 5 minutes until really light and fluffy. Beat in the eggs one at a time, then add the vanilla. Fold in the flour. Add enough milk to make a smooth, thickish mixture that will drop off the spoon when gently shaken. Spoon into the pudding basin.

STEP 3

Cut a piece of baking paper and a piece of foil the same size (big enough to cover the top of the pudding basin) and place one on top of the other. Hold them together and make a pleat in the centre (to allow the pudding to expand during cooking). Cover the top of the basin with the pleated paper and foil (foil on the outside) and tie under the rim of the basin with kitchen string to secure. Before cutting the string, take it up over the top to create a loose handle, then tie securely. Trim off any excess paper and foil.

STEP 4

Place the basin in a large pan and pour hot water into the pan until it reaches two-thirds of the way up the basin's sides. Cover and steam for 1½ hours. Allow the pudding to cool for about 5 minutes before turning out onto a serving plate and serving with custard or pouring cream.

CHEDDAR AND MUSTARD SAUSAGE ROLLS … ROAST PUMPKIN SCONES … HALLOWE'EN CUPCAKES … TOFFEE APPLES … PUMPKIN PIES … CHEESE STRAWS … CHOCOLATE CHIP COOKIES … GRAVADLAX … HAM HOCK TERRINE … TURKEY WITH STUFFING … CIDER-BAKED HAM … YULE LOG WITH CHESTNUT CREAM … MINCE PIES … ICED TREE BISCUITS … CHRISTMAS PUDDING … PANETTONE … CHEESE AND CARAWAY BISCUITS

SEASONAL OCCASIONS

Throughout the winter there are many holidays and traditions to celebrate, bringing cheer and merriment to the long, cold nights as well as really good grub.

Towards the end of autumn is Hallowe'en, with its ghosts and goblins and other scary fun. Trick-or-treating may seem a recent introduction, but it is thought to stem from the ancient tradition of baking and sharing 'soul cakes': peasant children would go from door to door collecting the cakes to pray for souls in purgatory. You could bake some cupcakes with two-tone frosting to share with your friends and children.

Hot on the heels of Hallowe'en comes Bonfire Night. Toffee apples are just the right treats to enjoy outdoors at the fireworks displays.

One of the most important celebrations of the whole calendar comes right at the end of the year – Christmas. There is an undeniable magic about it. Its spicy fragrances pervade the house and lift the spirits. True lovers of Yuletide can embrace the full works with the recipes in this chapter: there's the turkey and ham, of course, plus a deeply fruity Christmas pudding that can wait in the dark for its second steaming; the chocolate Yule log iced to resemble its wooden namesake; home-made mincemeat nestling inside butter-rich pastry shells; and pretty biscuits to dangle from a bauble-laden tree, piney scent mingling with the spices.

CHEDDAR AND MUSTARD SAUSAGE ROLLS

Succulent meat wrapped in flaky buttery pastry, served warm from the oven, sausage rolls are great for parties. Always make twice as many as you think you will need, as they won't last long! If you want to make canapé-sized sausage rolls just cut them into bite-sized (2cm) pieces and cook for a few minutes less.

MAKES 12 SAUSAGE ROLLS

2 teaspoons fennel seeds

1 tablespoon olive oil

1 red onion, very finely chopped

70g mature Cheddar cheese, finely grated

500g good-quality pork sausage meat

a small bunch of fresh flat-leaf parsley, finely chopped

8–10 fresh sage leaves, finely chopped

1 tablespoon English mustard

500g all-butter puff pastry, thawed if frozen

plain flour, for dusting

1 medium egg, beaten

salt and black pepper

STEP 1

Toast the fennel seeds in a dry frying pan over a medium-low heat for a minute until they smell fragrant. Tip into a bowl. Heat the oil in the pan and gently fry the red onion for 10–15 minutes until soft and golden. Set aside to cool.

STEP 2

Add the onion, cheese, sausage meat, herbs and mustard to the bowl and mix well together. Season with salt and pepper. To check the seasoning, fry a bit of the mix in a little oil and taste. Add more salt and pepper if needed.

STEP 3

Roll out the pastry on a lightly floured surface to a large rectangle about 33 x 28cm. Cut this lengthways in half to make two 33 x 14cm strips.

STEP 4

With wet hands, divide the filling in half and roll each half into a 33cm log. Lay a log along the middle of each pastry strip. Brush the pastry edges with a little beaten egg, then fold over to enclose the filling and seal well (roll so the join is underneath). Using a floured sharp knife, cut each roll across into 6 equal pieces. Brush with the rest of the beaten egg, then chill for 20 minutes.

STEP 5

Heat the oven, with a baking sheet inside, to 220°C/425°F/gas 7. Lightly score the top of each sausage roll with a knife, then transfer to the hot baking sheet. Bake for 15–18 minutes until golden and risen. Cool a little before serving.

ROAST PUMPKIN SCONES

The flavours of pumpkin and sage with a little hit of cheese are sublime together. These scones are best eaten warm, smothered in butter. Try them for breakfast or serve with soup.

MAKES 8–9 SCONES

YOU WILL NEED: 1 X 6CM FLUTED CUTTER

200g pumpkin or squash flesh, cut into small pieces

a drizzle of olive oil

225g self-raising flour, plus extra for dusting

40g cold unsalted butter, diced, plus extra for greasing

25g Cheddar cheese, grated

leaves from a sprig of fresh sage, finely chopped

freshly grated nutmeg

60–100ml buttermilk

milk, for brushing

salt and black pepper

STEP 1

Heat the oven to 200°C/400°F/gas 6. Spread the pumpkin pieces in a roasting tray and drizzle with a little oil. Season with salt and pepper. Place in the heated oven and roast for 20–25 minutes until tender. Mash the pumpkin well in the roasting tray or a bowl, then leave to cool completely.

STEP 2

Grease a baking sheet with butter. Sift the flour and ½ teaspoon of salt into a bowl and add the butter. Using your fingertips, rub the butter into the flour until the mixture resembles breadcrumbs. Use a table knife to mix the mashed pumpkin into the flour mixture. Mix in the Cheddar, sage and a good grating of nutmeg, then add just enough of the buttermilk to bring together and make a soft dough.

STEP 3

Turn out onto a lightly floured worktop and knead briefly until smooth. Form the dough into a ball, then pat it out to about 3cm thickness. Stamp out scones with a 6cm fluted cutter, gathering up the trimmings and kneading them together to make more scones. Arrange on the greased baking sheet. Brush the top of the scones with milk.

STEP 4

Place in the heated oven and bake for about 12 minutes until risen and golden. Transfer to a wire rack to cool.

HALLOWE'EN CUPCAKES

It may seem a weird idea, but these cupcakes are made beautifully moist by adding grated raw squash to the mix. No one will be able to guess what the secret ingredient is! You can experiment with different vegetables – try raw beetroot or parsnip in place of the squash. The cupcakes have a fun and funky spiralled two-tone frosting but you could ice them individually with orange or chocolate.

MAKES 18 CUPCAKES

YOU WILL NEED: 3 X 6-HOLE MUFFIN TINS;
AN ELECTRIC MIXER; 3 DISPOSABLE PIPING BAGS;
A LARGE STAR-SHAPED NOZZLE

225g unsalted butter, softened

225g caster sugar

3 medium eggs

150ml soured cream

225g self-raising flour

1 teaspoon baking powder

125g butternut squash flesh, coarsely grated

1 teaspoon vanilla extract

100g chocolate chips

FOR THE FROSTING

200g unsalted butter, softened

200g cream cheese

200g icing sugar, sifted

2–3 tablespoons cocoa powder

orange food colouring (the pastes from cake craft shops are the best)

a drop of orange extract

STEP 1
Heat the oven to 180°C/350°F/gas 4. Line three 6-hole muffin tins with paper cases.

STEP 2
Beat the butter with the sugar using an electric mixer (free-standing or hand-held) for about 4–5 minutes until really light and fluffy. Gradually add the eggs, beating after each addition, then add the soured cream. Fold in the flour and baking powder. Stir through the grated squash, vanilla and chocolate chips.

STEP 3
Spoon the mixture into the paper cases (an ice cream scoop is good for this, to ensure you add the same amount to each case). Place in the heated oven and bake for 15–20 minutes until the cupcakes are golden and a skewer inserted into the centre comes out clean. Remove the cupcakes to a wire rack and leave to cool.

STEP 4

For the frosting, beat together the butter and cream cheese until evenly combined. Beat in the icing sugar, then divide between 2 bowls. Add the cocoa powder to one bowl, and some orange food colouring and a drop of orange extract to the other. Mix the additions into the 2 frostings.

STEP 5

Take 3 disposable piping bags. Snip the end off one and insert a large star-shaped nozzle. Fill the second piping bag with the cocoa frosting and the third bag with the orange frosting. Snip the end off each of the 2 filled piping bags, then slip them inside the piping bag with the nozzle, making sure the snipped end of both bags goes inside the nozzle. You can now squeeze the outside bag to get a two-tone frosting effect.

STEP 6

Pipe the frosting over each cupcake, starting at the outside edge and moving inwards in a spiral.

TOFFEE APPLES

There is a childish pleasure in biting into the sweet crisp shell of a toffee apple to the juicy flesh beneath, especially if you are eagerly awaiting a spectacular display of fireworks. Although called 'toffee' apples, they are actually coated with a simple caramel rather than the softer, more fudge-like toffee. If you want to re-create the treats of fairgrounds, add a few drops of red food colouring to your caramel.

MAKES 8 TOFFEE APPLES

YOU WILL NEED: 8 LOLLIPOP STICKS (OR WOODEN SKEWERS); A SUGAR THERMOMETER

8 crunchy eating apples

500g caster sugar

100ml water

1 teaspoon white wine or malt vinegar

½ teaspoon flaky sea salt

3 tablespoons golden syrup

STEP 1

Place the apples in a heatproof bowl and pour over boiling water from the kettle. Immediately drain and rinse under cold running water. (This is to remove any grease or wax that would stop the toffee sticking.) Push a lollipop stick (or wooden skewer) into each apple. Line a large baking sheet with baking paper.

STEP 2

Put the sugar and measured water in a deep pan and heat gently, stirring to dissolve the sugar. Add the vinegar, salt and golden syrup, stir to combine and bring to the boil. Boil, without stirring, until the toffee reaches 140°C on a sugar thermometer (this is the hard crack stage). If you don't have a thermometer you can test by dropping a little of the toffee into a bowl of cold water; it should harden instantly and be very brittle when you remove it. If it is still squishable then continue to boil and test again.

STEP 3

When the toffee has reached the right temperature, remove the pan from the heat. Working quickly, hold each apple by its stick and dip into the toffee, rotating the apple to make sure it is covered all over. As each apple is dipped, place it on the lined baking sheet. Leave to cool and harden. (If the toffee in the pan starts to firm up before you have dipped all the apples, return it to the heat to soften to a dipping consistency.)

PUMPKIN PIES

An American tradition that has crossed the Atlantic, pumpkin pie is becoming an autumnal favourite here too. Evaporated milk gives the filling a light, creamy texture and the spices add a wonderful fragrance. In the US pumpkin for pies comes from a tin, which is sadly not readily available here, so we use fresh pumpkin instead – but not just any old pumpkin. Many have a watery flesh that isn't very flavoursome; these are much better used as Hallowe'en lanterns. Look out for what are called cooking or culinary pumpkins in supermarkets, or use a firm squash such as butternut or onion.

MAKES 6 PIES

YOU WILL NEED: A FOOD PROCESSOR, BLENDER OR HAND BLENDER; A 12CM PLAIN ROUND CUTTER; 6 X 10CM FLUTED TART TINS

400g cooking/culinary pumpkin or butternut squash

1 x quantity Sweet Shortcrust Pastry (see page 182)

plain flour, for dusting

90ml maple syrup

1 teaspoon ground ginger

½ teaspoon ground cinnamon

a pinch of ground cloves

1 tablespoon dark rum

2 medium eggs, beaten

30ml whipping cream

85ml evaporated milk

STEP 1

Heat the oven to 200°C/400°F/gas 6. Cut the pumpkin in half (cut a butternut squash lengthways in half) and remove the seeds and fibres, then cut into wedges. Spread out on a baking sheet. Place in the heated oven and roast for about 30 minutes until tender.

STEP 2

Remove from the oven (turn the oven off for now). When cool enough to handle, scoop the pumpkin flesh from the skin and place in a food processor or blender (or in a bowl if you want to use a hand blender). Blend to a smooth purée. Spoon the purée into a large meshed sieve set over a bowl and leave to drain off any excess moisture as it cools.

STEP 3

Roll out the pastry on a lightly floured surface to just less than the thickness of a pound coin. Cut out 6 rounds using a 12cm plain round cutter and use to line six 10cm fluted tart tins. Chill for 20 minutes.

STEP 4

Heat the oven to 200°C/400°F/gas 6. Line each tart case with baking paper and fill with baking beans or rice. Set them on a baking sheet. Place in the heated oven and bake blind for 12 minutes.

Remove the baking paper and beans or rice, then return to the oven and bake for a further 3–4 minutes until the tart cases are golden and sandy-feeling to the touch. Turn the oven down to 180°C/350°F/gas 4.

STEP 5

You will have about 350g of cooled, drained pumpkin purée now. Place it in a bowl with the maple syrup, spices, rum and eggs and mix together. Gradually stir in the cream and evaporated milk to make a thick double cream consistency. Pour into the tart cases.

STEP 6

Place in the heated oven and bake for about 15–20 minutes until the filling is just set but with a slight wobble. Allow the pies to cool in the tins for 10 minutes before removing to cool completely on a wire rack.

CHEESE STRAWS
FOR SOUP

Is there anything more delicious than a cheese straw with a warming bowl of soup? You can make a really quick and easy version with puff pastry (by cutting it into strips, brushing with melted butter and covering with grated cheese, then twisting and baking), but this version with short, crumbly pastry is worth every second it takes to make.

MAKES ABOUT 50 STRAWS

225g plain flour, plus extra for dusting

good pinch of salt

75g cold lard, cut into small pieces

75g cold butter, cut into small pieces, plus extra for greasing

50g Parmesan cheese, freshly grated

50g pecorino cheese, grated

½ teaspoon English mustard powder

good pinch of cayenne pepper

1–2 tablespoons iced water

1 egg, beaten

STEP 1

Put the flour in a bowl with the salt. Add the lard and butter and rub into the flour with your fingertips until the mixture resembles coarse breadcrumbs. Stir in all but a handful of the cheeses, the mustard powder and cayenne pepper. Add just enough iced water to bring the mixture together into a firm dough. Wrap in clingfilm and chill for 30 minutes.

STEP 2

Heat the oven to 200°C/400°F/gas 6, and lightly grease a baking sheet with butter. Roll out the pastry on a lightly floured surface to 5mm thick. Brush with beaten egg and sprinkle with the remaining cheese. Cut into strips 1cm wide and 10cm long. Arrange on the baking sheet.

STEP 3

Place in the heated oven and bake for 10–15 minutes until golden brown. Transfer to a wire rack to cool briefly, then serve warm.

CHOCOLATE CHIP COOKIES

Cookies are NOT the same as biscuits —
cookies have a chewy yet crumbly texture
that sets them apart from their more British
counterpart. A chocolate chip cookie is hard to
beat. Try these with creamy hot chocolate on a
cold winter's night.

MAKES 12 LARGE COOKIES

YOU WILL NEED: AN ELECTRIC MIXER (HAND-HELD)

175g unsalted butter, softened

100g golden caster sugar

50g light brown muscovado sugar

1 large egg

50g hazelnuts, finely chopped but not ground

225g self-raising flour

¼ teaspoon salt

½ teaspoon bicarbonate of soda

100g dark chocolate, finely chopped

STEP 1

Heat the oven to 190°C/375°F/gas 5. Put the butter and 2 types of sugar in a bowl and beat with an electric mixer until creamy.

STEP 2

Beat in the egg, hazelnuts, flour, salt and bicarbonate of soda, then add the chocolate and mix well.

STEP 3

Shape into 12 equal-sized balls. Place on a non-stick baking sheet, spaced well apart (to allow for spreading during baking), then flatten each ball a little. Chill for 30 minutes.

STEP 4

Place in the heated oven and bake for about 10 minutes until golden. Leave on the baking sheet to firm up for 5 minutes, then transfer to a wire rack to cool completely.

GRAVADLAX

One of the greatest Scandinavian dishes, this is so simple to make but utterly wonderful and luxurious to eat. It's perfect at Christmastime, but is also fabulous at any other time of year. You can vary the flavours easily. For example, make a beetroot cure by adding coarsely grated raw beetroot to the marinade and using vodka instead of aquavit. You could also replace the juniper with a few crushed black peppercorns. Beetroot gives the gravadlax an amazing colour and lovely earthy flavour.

MAKES ABOUT 1.4KG

2 sides (whole fillets) of salmon, 800–900g each

100g flaky sea salt

150g caster sugar

10 juniper berries, lightly crushed

60ml aquavit

175g fresh dill, finely chopped

STEP 1

Make sure all the pin bones have been removed from the salmon. Place a double layer of clingfilm on the worktop – the clingfilm needs to be big enough to wrap both the pieces of salmon once they are sandwiched together. Place one of the salmon fillets, skin-side down, on the clingfilm.

STEP 2

Mix together the salt, sugar and juniper in a bowl. Add the aquavit and chopped dill and mix well. Spread the mixture evenly over the fillet that is on the clingfilm. Top with the other fillet, flesh-side down, to form a sandwich.

STEP 3

Wrap the fish tightly in the clingfilm and place in a dish that's just big enough to hold the parcel snugly. Set a small chopping board that fits inside the dish on top of the parcel and weigh it down (full tins of food are ideal). Place in the fridge to marinate for 24–48 hours, turning the parcel and draining off any liquid that collects in the dish every 12 hours or so.

STEP 4

Unwrap the salmon and rinse off the cure under cold running water. Pat dry with kitchen paper. The gravadlax can now be sliced very thinly and eaten. It will keep, wrapped in fresh clingfilm, in the fridge for up to a week. Serve on rye bread with soured cream and dill, or on warm blinis with a squeeze of lemon and topped with a dollop of crème fraîche.

HAM HOCK TERRINE

This terrine is a beautiful mosaic of pink ham, green herbs and golden apple jelly. It's a great dish to have in the fridge over the festive season. Serve it as a starter or for lunch.

SERVES 8

YOU WILL NEED: A 1.5 LITRE LOAF TIN OR TERRINE

2.5kg unsmoked ham hocks on the bone, soaked overnight in cold water

1 onion, quartered

1 large carrot, cut into chunks

2 celery sticks, cut into 4cm lengths

2 fresh bay leaves

5 sprigs of fresh thyme

2 teaspoons coriander seeds

8 black peppercorns

4 tablespoons cider vinegar

500ml clear apple juice

70g cornichons, finely chopped

a large handful of fresh flat-leaf parsley, chopped

a small handful of fresh tarragon, chopped

2 gelatine sheets

black pepper

STEP 1
Drain the ham hocks, then place them in a large saucepan with the onion, carrot, celery, bay leaves, thyme, coriander seeds, peppercorns and vinegar. Pour over the apple juice and enough cold water to cover. Bring to the boil, then simmer very gently, uncovered, for 2–2½ hours until the meat is tender and will flake easily.

STEP 2
Leave the hocks to cool in the liquid for about 1 hour, then remove and set aside. Strain the liquid into a clean pan and boil vigorously until reduced to about 800ml. Remove from the heat.

STEP 3
Line a 1.5 litre loaf tin or terrine mould with a double layer of clingfilm. Remove the skin from the ham hocks, then shred the meat into large chunks. Place in a large bowl and add the cornichons and chopped herbs. Mix well and season with plenty of black pepper. Pack into the tin or mould and press down firmly.

STEP 4
Soak the gelatine in cold water for 5 minutes, then squeeze out excess water and add to the warm poaching liquid. Stir until melted. Slowly pour the liquid into the tin or mould, allowing it to settle around the meat. Cover with clingfilm and leave in the fridge overnight to set.

STEP 5
Cut the terrine into thick slices and serve with crusty sourdough bread and piccalilli or chutney.

ROAST TURKEY WITH CHESTNUT, PANCETTA AND PRUNE STUFFING

Nothing says Christmas to me like a golden roasted turkey with a succulent stuffing. An often-heard opinion is that turkey meat is dry and flavourless. So let's get one thing straight at the outset: there really is no excuse for a dry turkey. When cooked properly the meat is wonderfully juicy. The dark meat is particularly succulent. Because of its size you can rest your turkey for up to an hour and it will still be piping hot, leaving you loads of time to finish the rest of the Christmas lunch.

SERVES 8, WITH LEFTOVERS

1 x 5–6kg turkey (take it out of the fridge at least 45 minutes before cooking)

25g unsalted butter, softened

finely grated zest of 1 lemon

fresh bay leaves and rosemary sprigs, for the cavity of the turkey

FOR THE STUFFING

1 tablespoon olive oil

1 x 150g piece pancetta, finely chopped

40g unsalted butter

1 small onion, finely chopped

2 large garlic cloves, crushed

60g fresh breadcrumbs

175g peeled cooked chestnuts (whole)

100ml chicken or turkey stock

200g pork sausage meat

150g pork mince

100g soft dried prunes, finely chopped

a small bunch of fresh parsley, finely chopped

8 fresh sage leaves, finely chopped

freshly grated nutmeg

salt and black pepper

STEP 1

First make the stuffing. Heat the oil in a frying pan over a medium heat and fry the pancetta until starting to crisp. Remove to a bowl using a slotted spoon. Reduce the heat, add half the butter to the pan, then add the onion and fry gently for 10 minutes until softened. Add the garlic and cook for a further 2 minutes. Add the onion and garlic to the pancetta, then mix in the breadcrumbs.

STEP 2

Heat the remaining butter in the frying pan and fry the chestnuts for a couple of minutes. Add the stock and bring to the boil, then bubble until almost all of the stock has been absorbed and the chestnuts are coated in buttery juices. Break them up with the back of a wooden spoon, then add to the pancetta and onion mixture in the bowl. Leave to cool completely.

STEP 3

Add the sausage meat, mince, prunes and herbs to the bowl and mix well. Season generously with nutmeg, salt and pepper.

STEP 4

Heat the oven to 200°C/400°F/gas 6. Untruss your turkey. Working from the neck end, gently ease your fingers under the skin to separate it from the flesh. Take care not to tear the skin. Fill the pocket you've made with the stuffing, then pull the skin back over, smoothing it out. Secure the skin underneath with a skewer if you need to. Tie the legs of the turkey together.

STEP 5

Mix the butter with the lemon zest and smear all over the skin. Season the bird with salt and pepper, then weigh to calculate the cooking time: allow 20 minutes per kg, plus an extra 30 minutes. Stuff bay leaves and rosemary into the body cavity. Set the bird in a large roasting tin.

STEP 6

Place in the heated oven and roast for 30 minutes, then turn the oven down to 180°C/350°F/gas 4. Continue roasting for the rest of the calculated cooking time, basting occasionally with the juices in the tin. If the turkey starts to get too brown, cover it loosely with foil. To test if the turkey is cooked, pierce the thickest part of the thigh with a skewer: the juices that run out should be clear. Leave the turkey to rest, loosely covered with foil, for 30 minutes before carving.

SPICED CIDER-BAKED CHRISTMAS HAM

There is something so delicious about a freshly cooked ham, hot from the oven, when the fat is all sticky and the meat juicy and delicious. This ham will feed a crowd, with plenty of leftovers that will never go to waste: eat the ham cold with a baked potato or chips; slice it for pies, risottos and pastas; toss it through lentils or a salad; use in soups…

SERVES 8, WITH LEFTOVERS

1 large onion, quartered

3 fresh bay leaves

2 star anise

1 cinnamon stick

6 black peppercorns

5 allspice berries

1.5 litres medium-dry cider

1 x 6kg unsmoked ham on the bone, soaked overnight in cold water, then drained

15 cloves

2 tablespoons golden syrup

3 tablespoons black treacle

2 teaspoons ground ginger

a good pinch of cayenne pepper

2–3 tablespoons demerara sugar

STEP 1
Heat the oven to 120°C/250°F/gas ½. Put the onion, bay leaves, star anise, cinnamon stick, peppercorns and allspice in a large, deep, flameproof roasting tray. Pour in the cider, then put a rack in the tray. Set the ham on the rack. Cover the tin with a tent of foil, sealing it well.

STEP 2
Set the tray on the hob and bring the cider to the boil. Simmer for 15 minutes, then transfer the tray to the oven. Leave to cook for 12 hours.

STEP 3
Remove the tray from the oven. Now you can either set the ham aside until it is cool enough to handle and then continue with the final glazing straightaway, or you can leave the ham to cool completely and then finish it the next day.

STEP 4
Turn the oven up (or on) to 180°C/350°F/gas 4. Using a sharp knife, carefully peel the skin away from the cooked ham, leaving as much of the fat on the ham as you can. Score the fat in a criss-cross pattern and press the cloves into the crosses.

STEP 5
Mix the golden syrup with the treacle. Using a spoon, drizzle this mixture all over the fat of the ham. Sprinkle with the ginger, cayenne pepper and sugar. Roast for 20 minutes (or, if cooled and being reheated to serve the next day, for 45–60 minutes) until covered with a sticky glaze and piping hot throughout.

YULE LOG WITH CHESTNUT CREAM

In the days when people had large hearths the wooden Yule Log was an important part of Christmas. The enormous log would be blessed and set alight on Christmas Eve, then kept burning for the twelve days of Christmas to bring luck to the household. These days, it is the edible – and seriously delicious – chocolate Yule log, or Bûche de Nöel in French, that is a traditional part of our Christmas feasts. Don't worry if your roulade cracks as you roll it, as it so often does – this will add to its charm. If you like, spread chocolate buttercream over the roulade and swirl bark-like patterns with a fork so the log resembles its wooden namesake.

SERVES 8

YOU WILL NEED: A 22 X 32CM SWISS ROLL TIN; A HAND-HELD ELECTRIC MIXER

unsalted butter for greasing

200g plain chocolate (50% cocoa solids), broken up

6 large eggs, separated

200g caster sugar, plus extra for sprinkling

200ml double cream

1 teaspoon vanilla extract

100g sweet chestnut purée

75g cooked peeled chestnuts, chopped

icing sugar, for dusting

STEP 1
Heat the oven to 180°C/350°F/gas 4. Grease a 22 x 32cm Swiss roll tin with butter, then line the base and sides with baking paper.

STEP 2
Put the chocolate in a heatproof bowl, set over a pan of barely simmering water (make sure the base of the bowl doesn't touch the water) and leave to melt gently. Stir until smooth, then remove the bowl from the pan and leave the chocolate to cool a little.

STEP 3
Meanwhile, whisk the egg yolks with the caster sugar in a large bowl using a hand-held electric mixer for 4–5 minutes until pale, thick and creamy. Whisk in the slightly cooled melted chocolate. In a separate bowl, whisk the egg whites to soft peaks. Stir a quarter of the whisked whites into the chocolate mixture to loosen it, then gently fold in the remaining whites using a large metal spoon, until just combined.

STEP 4
Pour the mixture into the lined tin and smooth out to the sides and corners to fill evenly. Place in the heated oven and bake for 20–25 minutes until the sponge is springy to the touch and starting to come away from the sides of the tin. Remove from the oven, set the tin on a wire rack and leave to cool for 10 minutes.

STEP 5

Place a sheet of baking paper on the worktop and sprinkle with caster sugar. Turn out the sponge onto the sugared paper. Peel off the lining paper, then cover the sponge with a clean sheet of baking paper and a damp tea towel. Leave to cool for 1–2 hours.

STEP 6

For the filling, whip the cream until it just holds its shape. Fold in the vanilla extract and chestnut purée and whisk again until thick. Carefully fold in the chopped chestnuts.

STEP 7

Trim the edges off the sponge, then spread the chestnut cream evenly over the surface. Carefully roll up the sponge from one short end, using the sugared paper to help you. Place the roulade on a serving plate and dust with icing sugar before serving.

MINCE PIES

These pies will freeze brilliantly — freeze them uncooked, in their tins, until solid, then keep in a freezer bag; when you want them, pop back in the tins and bake from frozen.

MAKES 24 MINCE PIES

YOU WILL NEED: STERILISED JARS (SEE PAGE 287); AN 8CM AND A 7CM FLUTED ROUND CUTTER; 2 X 12-HOLE MINCE PIE TIN

2 x quantities Shortcrust for Mince Pies (see page 145)

plain flour, for dusting

milk, for brushing and glazing

caster sugar, for sprinkling

FOR THE MINCEMEAT

75ml brandy

grated zest and juice of 1 orange

500g mixed dried fruit (raisins, sultanas and currants)

2 large Bramley apples, cored and coarsely grated

125g beef suet, shredded

200g light soft brown sugar

100g chopped mixed candied peel

75g flaked almonds

1 tablespoon ground mixed spice

grated zest of 1 lemon

STEP 1
To make the mincemeat, heat the brandy with the orange zest and juice in a small pan. Pour over the dried fruit in a large mixing bowl and leave for a couple of hours so the fruit can absorb the liquid.

STEP 2
Heat the oven to 100°C/200°F/gas very low. Mix all the remaining ingredients for the mincemeat into the fruit mixture, then transfer to an ovenproof dish. Cover the dish and place in the heated oven to cook, stirring regularly, for 1–2 hours until all the suet has melted and is coating the fruit. Spoon the mincemeat into sterilised jars, seal and leave to cool.

STEP 3
When you're ready to make the mince pies, heat the oven to 200°C/400°F/gas 6. Roll out the pastry on a lightly floured worktop to the thickness of a 20p coin. With an 8cm fluted cutter, cut out 24 rounds and use to line two 12-hole mince pie tins. Dollop a heaped teaspoon of mincemeat into each case.

STEP 4
Re-roll the trimmings, then cut out 24 lids using a 7cm fluted cutter. Brush the edges of the mince pie cases with milk and put the lids in place. Use your fingers to gently press the edges together to seal.

STEP 5
Brush the pastry lids with milk and pierce a hole in the top of each one. Place in the heated oven and bake for 12–15 minutes until the pastry is golden brown. Remove the pies from the tin, sprinkle with caster sugar and serve warm.

ICED TREE BISCUITS

These lightly spiced little biscuits make great edible Christmas tree decorations, tied with a festive ribbon. Covered in pretty icing and sparkles, they will twinkle and shine until small (or grown-up) hands pluck them from the boughs and devour them.

MAKES 10–18 BISCUITS, DEPENDING ON CUTTERS

YOU WILL NEED: A HAND-HELD ELECTRIC MIXER; DECORATIVE SHAPED BISCUIT CUTTERS; A SMALL DISPOSABLE PIPING BAG

100g unsalted butter, softened

75g light soft brown sugar

2 tablespoons runny honey

1 medium egg, lightly beaten

200g plain flour, sifted

½ teaspoon baking powder

2 teaspoons ground ginger

1 teaspoon ground cinnamon

pinch of salt

75g stem ginger, finely chopped

FOR THE ICING

500g ready-made Royal Icing sugar

75–100ml lemon juice

blue food colouring

lustre, sparkles or dragées, to decorate

STEP 1

Whisk the butter with the sugar using a hand-held electric mixer for 4–5 minutes until really light and fluffy. Whisk in the honey and egg. Combine the flour, baking powder, spices and salt in another bowl, then sift into the butter mixture and stir until incorporated. Fold through the stem ginger. Bring together with your hands into a soft dough, kneading briefly until smooth.

STEP 2

Roll out the dough between 2 sheets of clingfilm to the thickness of a pound coin. Transfer to a tray and place in the fridge to firm up for an hour.

STEP 3

Heat the oven to 180°C/350°F/gas 4. Cut out your biscuits using decorative biscuit cutters, such as stars, snowflakes or bauble shapes. Re-roll the trimmings to make as many biscuits as possible.

STEP 4

Use a palette knife to transfer the biscuits to a baking sheet lined with baking paper. Place in the heated oven and bake for 10–15 minutes until the biscuits are browning at the edges. Remove from the oven. Use a piping nozzle or skewer to pierce a hole in one corner of each biscuit. Leave to cool on the baking sheet.

STEP 5

To make the icing, sift the icing sugar into a bowl and whisk in enough lemon juice to give a stiff piping consistency. Add a tiny drop of blue food colouring to make the icing look bright white.

STEP 6

Spoon the icing into a small disposable piping bag and snip off the tip to make a very small hole (or use a fine plain nozzle in your piping bag). Decorate your biscuits with the icing. You can either pipe intricate patterns on the biscuits, or pipe an outline around the edge and leave to set for 10 minutes before flooding the centre of the biscuit with thinned-down icing. Decorate the flooded biscuits with lustre, sparkles or dragées.

STEP 7

Once the icing has set, thread pretty ribbons through the holes so you can hang the biscuits on your tree.

CHRISTMAS PUDDING

A Christmas pudding should be rich, dark and packed full of boozy fruits. Make yours at least a month in advance (or up to 6 months), then let it mature in a cool, dark place until Christmas Day. Don't forget to make a wish as you stir the pudding mixture!

SERVES 8

YOU WILL NEED: A 1.5 LITRE PUDDING BASIN

butter for greasing

350g mixed raisins and sultanas

125g each prunes and dried apricots, finely chopped

75g dried apple, finely chopped

grated zest of 1 large orange

1 eating apple, peeled, cored and grated

50g fresh white breadcrumbs

100g blanched almonds, chopped

50g ground almonds

2 tablespoons ground mixed spice

100g shredded suet

100g light muscovado sugar

50g dark muscovado sugar

3 medium eggs, beaten

100ml Calvados or brandy, plus extra to serve

STEP 1

Grease a 1.5 litre pudding basin with butter. Put all the ingredients in a large mixing bowl and mix together until thoroughly combined. Spoon the mixture into the pudding basin.

STEP 2

Cut a square each of foil and baking paper, large enough to fit over the basin with some overhang. Put the two squares together. If your basin is quite full, fold a pleat in the centre of the foil/paper square to give the pudding some space to rise. Place, paper-side down, over the basin and secure with string under the rim (take the string up over the top to make a loose handle before cutting the string). Trim off any excess paper/foil.

STEP 3

Put an upturned saucer in the base of a deep pan. Set the pudding basin on top. Pour boiling water into the pan to come halfway up the sides of the basin. Cover and steam for 5 hours, topping up the water as needed. Using the string handle, carefully lift the basin out of the pan. Cool, then cover with clean paper and foil before storing.

STEP 4

To reheat for serving, steam for 1–1½ hours until piping hot throughout. Remove from the pan and turn out the pudding on to a plate. Warm a splash of Calvados or brandy in a small pan, then pour over the pudding and set alight. Bring to the table while flaming (let the flames die out before spooning out servings).

PANETTONE

Vanilla-scented and laden with juicy fruit, panettone is a buttery cake-bread akin to French brioche. There are many legends surrounding the origins of panettone, one of which says that it dates back to the 14th century and comes from the Milanaise 'pan dei ton', which means luxury bread.

MAKES 1 LARGE PANETTONE

YOU WILL NEED: AN ELECTRIC MIXER (PREFERABLY LARGE, FREE-STANDING); A 20CM ROUND LOOSE-BOTTOMED CAKE TIN OR PANETTONE MOULD

80g each raisins and sultanas

3 tablespoons dark rum

200g unsalted butter, softened, plus extra for greasing

100g golden caster sugar

2 teaspoons vanilla extract

3 large eggs, beaten, plus 1 egg white for glazing

grated zest of 1 large orange

grated zest of 1 lemon

600g type 00 flour, plus extra for dusting

2 teaspoons salt

pinch of freshly grated nutmeg

25g fresh yeast OR 2 x 7g sachets fast-action
   dried yeast

200ml full-fat milk, warmed until tepid

100g chopped candied citrus peel

icing sugar, for dusting

STEP 1

Put the raisins and sultanas in a small pan with the rum and heat gently for 1–2 minutes. Set aside to cool and allow the fruit to absorb the rum.

STEP 2

In a large bowl, beat the butter with the caster sugar and vanilla using an electric mixer for 5 minutes until light and fluffy. Gradually beat in the eggs. Beat in the orange and lemon zests.

STEP 3

Sift the flour, salt and nutmeg into a large bowl. If using fresh yeast, add to the warm milk and stir until dissolved, then set aside for a few minutes so the yeast can activate and froth the milk. If using dried yeast, sprinkle it over the flour. Make a well in the centre of the flour and pour in the milk/yeast mixture or warm milk. Quickly mix the liquid with the flour. Add the whisked butter and egg mixture and fold in with a large spatula to make a soft, sticky dough.

STEP 4

Turn out the dough onto a floured worktop and knead for 10–15 minutes until smooth and elastic. Form into a ball, then place in a lightly greased bowl and cover with clingfilm. Leave in a warm place to rise for 1½ hours until doubled in size.

STEP 5

Tip the risen dough onto the floured surface. Knead for a minute or so, then knead in the raisins, sultanas and candied peel until evenly distributed. Form the dough into a smooth ball and place it in a 20cm round loose-bottomed cake tin or a panettone mould. Cover loosely with clingfilm. Leave in a warm place to rise for 2 hours until the dough has tripled in size.

STEP 6

Heat the oven to 200°C/400°F/gas 6. Brush the top of the panettone with egg white. Wrap a double layer of baking paper around the outside of the cake tin or panettone mould – the paper should rise 10cm above the rim of the tin or mould. Secure the paper collar with string. Set the tin on a baking sheet.

STEP 7

Place in the heated oven and bake for 15 minutes, then reduce the temperature to 180°C/350°F/gas 4 and bake for a further 40–45 minutes. Cover with foil if the panettone starts to take on too much colour. It's ready when a skewer inserted in the centre comes out clean.

STEP 8

If your panettone has been baked in a tin, cool for 5 minutes before turning out onto a wire rack to cool completely. If in a panettone mould, leave to cool in the mould set on a wire rack. Dredge with icing sugar before serving in slices.

CHEESE AND CARAWAY BISCUITS

Little cheesy biscuits are always a bit hit, whether you serve them still warm from the oven as a pre-supper nibble with a glass of something cold, or with cheese afterwards. Hints of caraway and walnut add a little something special to an otherwise classic cheese biscuit.

MAKES 50–60 BISCUITS

YOU WILL NEED: A SMALL FOOD PROCESSOR

25g walnuts

150g plain flour, plus extra for dusting

good pinch of flaky sea salt

½–1 teaspoon cayenne pepper

1 teaspoon caraway seeds, lightly crushed

100g cold unsalted butter, diced

50g mature Cheddar cheese, finely grated

75g Parmesan cheese, freshly grated

milk, for brushing

black pepper

STEP 1

Grind the walnuts in a small food processor. Tip them into a bowl and add the flour, salt, cayenne, caraway seeds and a good grinding of black pepper. Add the diced butter and rub into the flour with your fingertips until the mixture resembles fine breadcrumbs.

STEP 2

Add the grated cheeses and mix them in with a flat-bladed knife to make a dough – you may need to add a tiny splash of cold water to bring all the ingredients together.

STEP 3

Tip the dough out onto a lightly floured worktop and knead for a few seconds. Roll into a log shape roughly 5cm in diameter. Wrap in clingfilm and chill in the fridge for a couple of hours until firm. (The log of dough can be kept in the fridge for up to 10 days, and also freezes really well.)

STEP 4

Heat the oven to 180°C/350°/gas 4. Unwrap the log of dough and cut across into discs about 5mm thick. Arrange these on baking sheets lined with baking paper, spacing the biscuits well apart. Brush with milk, then place in the heated oven and bake for 12–15 minutes until crisp and golden.

STEP 5

Leave to cool and firm up on the baking sheets for a couple of minutes, then transfer to a wire rack. Once completely cold, store the biscuits in an airtight box. They will keep for 4–5 days.

BEETROOT AND CHOCOLATE
BROWNIES … PEAR AND ALMOND
TRAYBAKE … STICKY CLEMENTINE
CAKE … PEANUT BUTTER BROWNIE
… WATERCRESS AND FETA
MUFFINS … APPLE AND SOURED
CREAM MUFFINS … CORNBREAD
… SODA BREAD … WHITE ROLLS
… SOURDOUGH STARTER …
SOURDOUGH BREAD … BANANA
AND CHOCOLATE LOAF … STICKY
GINGERBREAD … CHILLI AND
PINEAPPLE CAKE … MALT LOAF
… TEA CAKES … FRUIT CAKE …
POPPYSEED LOAF … HOME-MADE
PIZZAS

BREADS & BAKES

*For anyone who has never made bread, now is the time to start.
A bread dough is a forgiving beast – it doesn't mind being
manhandled, left for hours and then wonkily shaped, as
long as it is made with love.*

It can come in many guises: a soft and pillowy shape with a poppyseed-dusted crust, designed to be torn into pieces with your hands; a crusty, tangy, open-textured sourdough round; a base for a pizza; and spicy little glazed discs laden with dried fruit and peel. Then there are quickly made soda bread and cornbread, which taste as good as any of their yeasty cousins.

Cold weather seems the right time for baking cakes too. What is it that is so utterly irresistible about them? Is it the crumb, so moist and tender, or the icing, if there is one, just sweet and thick enough to coat? A malt loaf, muffins, a drizzle cake, brownies, gingerbread and a sumptuous fruit cake – all so tempting. Cake is not about need but about indulgence, about giving in to a little slice of pure joy.

BEETROOT AND CHOCOLATE BROWNIES

A really good brownie should be dense, gooey and intensely chocolatey. The beetroot added to the mix here gives the brownies a beautiful reddish hue and a subtle earthy flavour that complements the chocolate.

CUTS INTO 16 SQUARES

YOU WILL NEED: A 20CM SQUARE CAKE TIN

2 raw beetroots, about 200g total weight (unpeeled)

150g unsalted butter, softened, plus extra for greasing

1 teaspoon vanilla extract

200g dark chocolate (70% cocoa solids), broken up

170g light muscovado sugar

100g golden caster sugar

a pinch of salt

2 large eggs, beaten

160g plain flour

cocoa powder, for dusting

STEP 1

Heat the oven to 180°C/350°F/gas 4. Wrap the beetroot individually in foil. Place in the heated oven and bake for 30–40 minutes until tender. Remove (leave the oven on) and set aside until cool enough to handle, then peel them. Coarsely grate them into a bowl and set aside.

STEP 2

Grease a 20cm square cake tin with butter, then line the base and sides with baking paper. Put the butter, vanilla, dark chocolate, muscovado and caster sugars and salt in a large heatproof bowl. Set over a pan of barely simmering water (make sure the base of the bowl does not touch the water) and heat gently until the chocolate and butter have melted and the sugars have dissolved, stirring occasionally. Remove from the heat. Mix in the eggs and grated beetroot, then fold in the flour.

STEP 3

Spoon the mixture into the prepared tin, smoothing the top with the back of the spoon. Place in the heated oven and bake for 25 minutes until the top of the brownie cake is firm to the touch, but it's still a little bit gooey in the centre (test with a skewer).

STEP 4

Remove from the oven and cool in the tin for at least 20 minutes before turning out. Once completely cold, dust with cocoa powder, then cut into squares.

PEAR AND ALMOND TRAYBAKE

Pears and almonds make a great combination, classic in tarts and pastries. Here they flavour a fantastic soft-textured sponge that is perfect for teatime. Or you could serve it warm with a splodge of crème fraîche as a pudding.

CUTS INTO 12 SQUARES

YOU WILL NEED: A 30 X 23CM TRAYBAKE TIN OR CAKE TIN; A HAND-HELD ELECTRIC MIXER

175g unsalted butter, softened, plus extra for greasing

190g golden caster sugar

3 large eggs, lightly beaten

1 teaspoon vanilla extract

1 x 142ml carton buttermilk

180g self-raising flour

175g ground almonds

finely grated zest of 1 lemon

a squeeze of lemon juice

2 large, ripe but firm pears, peeled, cored and cut into small bite-sized chunks

50g flaked almonds

STEP 1
Heat the oven to 180°C/350°F/gas 4. Grease a 30 x 23cm traybake tin or cake tin with butter, then line the base and sides with baking paper.

STEP 2
Beat the butter with the sugar using a hand-held electric mixer for 4–5 minutes until light and fluffy. Gradually add the eggs, beating well after each addition. Add the vanilla extract and buttermilk and beat to incorporate. Sift the flour and ground almonds into the bowl. Fold in with the lemon zest and juice, then fold in the pears.

STEP 3
Spoon the mixture into the prepared tin. Sprinkle the flaked almonds over the surface. Place in the heated oven and bake for 40–45 minutes until golden and risen and a skewer inserted into the centre comes out clean (unless you've hit a bit of pear, of course!).

STEP 4
Remove from the oven and leave to cool for 20 minutes, then serve warm for a pudding. Or turn out onto a wire rack and allow to cool completely, to eat at teatime.

STICKY CLEMENTINE CAKE

The only fat in this flourless cake comes from almonds and eggs, yet it is moist, tender-textured and very moreish. The citrus syrup adds a sticky sweet finish, but if you love a frosting you can make a citrus icing instead, with icing sugar and clementine juice, to drizzle over the top.

SERVES 10

YOU WILL NEED: A FOOD PROCESSOR; A 23CM SPRINGFORM CAKE TIN

5 clementines

unsalted butter, for greasing

275g caster sugar

300g ground almonds

seeds from 8–10 cardamom pods, ground to a powder

1 teaspoon baking powder

2 teaspoons vanilla extract

6 large eggs, lightly beaten

juice of 1 lemon

1 cinnamon stick

STEP 1

Put 3 of the clementines in a pan of water, bring to the boil and simmer for about 2 hours until really tender. Drain the clementines. Cut them in half and pick out any pips, then blitz the fruit (skin and flesh) to a pulp in a food processor.

STEP 2

Heat the oven to 180°C/350°F/gas 4. Grease a 23cm springform cake tin with butter, then line the base with baking paper.

STEP 3

Combine 225g of the caster sugar, the almonds, cardamom and baking powder in a large bowl. Stir, then make a well in the centre. Mix the pulped clementines, vanilla extract and eggs in the well, then mix in the dry ingredients. Pour the mixture into the tin. Place in the heated oven and bake for 50–60 minutes until a skewer inserted into the centre of the cake comes out clean.

STEP 4

While the cake is baking, squeeze the juice from the remaining 2 clementines into a pan. Add the lemon juice and remaining 50g caster sugar. Heat gently until the sugar dissolves, then add the cinnamon stick and simmer for 3 minutes.

STEP 5

Remove the cake from the oven and pierce it in a few places with a skewer. Drizzle over the citrus syrup, then leave for 1 hour to soak in. Transfer the cake to a wire rack to cool completely. Serve with pouring cream.

PEANUT BUTTER AND WHITE CHOCOLATE BROWNIE

The combination of peanut butter and chocolate is well known. Not as dense as its darker chocolate counterpart, the white chocolate brownie, or blondie, has a more innocent, sweet appeal. Adding peanut butter to the brownies makes them completely irresistible.

CUTS INTO 16 SQUARES

YOU WILL NEED: A HAND-HELD ELECTRIC MIXER; 1 X 20CM SQUARE CAKE TIN

150g white chocolate, cut into pieces

125g unsalted butter, softened, plus extra for greasing

175g light brown muscovado sugar

1 teaspoon vanilla extract

100g crunchy peanut butter

2 large eggs, beaten

100g plain flour

1 teaspoon baking powder

STEP 1

Heat the oven to 180°C/350°F/gas 4. Grease a 20cm square cake tin with butter and line the base with baking paper. Put half the chocolate into a heatproof bowl, set over a pan of gently simmering water (check that the base of the bowl does not touch the water) and allow to melt slowly. Remove the bowl from the heat and set aside to cool a little while making the mixture.

STEP 2

Put the butter in a large mixing bowl and beat with a hand-held electric mixer until soft and creamy. Add the sugar, vanilla extract, remaining chopped chocolate and peanut butter and continue beating until the mixture is soft and fluffy. Gradually beat in the eggs.

STEP 3

Sift the flour and baking powder over the mixture, and spoon over the melted chocolate. Stir everything together thoroughly. Pour the mixture into the prepared tin.

STEP 4

Place in the heated oven and bake for about 35–40 minutes until firm to the touch but still soft in the centre (the brownies will continue to cook as they cool). Leave to cool almost completely before removing from the tin, using the paper to lift the brownie cake out. Cut into 16 squares. Eat warm or at room temperature.

WATERCRESS AND FETA MUFFINS

These little muffins are a great bake to have in your repertoire. Perfect for breakfast or brunch, or served alongside soup at lunchtime; there is no end to their usefulness. Buttermilk makes the muffins lovely and moist, and the flavours of watercress and feta go brilliantly together, but also try mixing up the flavours, using spinach and bacon or little pieces of chorizo, pecorino or blue cheese instead of feta. The options are endless.

MAKES 12 MUFFINS

YOU WILL NEED: 1 X 12-HOLE MUFFIN TIN

200g watercress

250g plain flour

½ teaspoon flaky sea salt

2 teaspoons baking powder

½ teaspoon bicarbonate of soda

75g strong Cheddar cheese, coarsely grated

75g feta cheese, crumbled

2 medium eggs, beaten

75g unsalted butter, melted and cooled

200ml buttermilk

50ml full-fat milk

STEP 1

Heat the oven to 200°C/400°F/gas 6, and line a 12-hole muffin tray with paper muffin cases. Put the watercress in a colander in the sink and wilt it by pouring over boiling water from the kettle. Refresh under running cold water, then squeeze handfuls to remove as much liquid as you can. Transfer the watercress to a chopping board and chop finely.

STEP 2

Mix the flour with the salt, baking powder and bicarbonate of soda in a large bowl. Reserve a small amount of the Cheddar, then add the rest and all the feta to the bowl and stir to mix in. In a separate bowl or large jug, mix together the beaten eggs, melted butter, buttermilk and milk. Pour the egg mixture over the ingredients in the large bowl and stir until just combined. Quickly fold in the cooled chopped watercress until everything is evenly distributed. The batter will be a bit lumpy.

STEP 3

Spoon the batter into the muffin cases, dividing it equally. Scatter the reserved Cheddar on top. Place in the heated oven and bake for 18–20 minutes until golden and risen, and a skewer inserted into the middle of a muffin comes out clean. Remove the muffins from the tin and place on a wire rack to cool. Serve warm or at room temperature.

APPLE AND SOURED CREAM MUFFINS

Apples always work well in cakes and puddings because as they are baking they release steam, making the sponge gloriously soft and moist inside. The sharp flavour of Bramley apples is the perfect foil to the sweetness of this muffin batter, and the chunks of fruit give little bites of texture.

MAKES 12 MUFFINS

YOU WILL NEED: A 12-HOLE MUFFIN TRAY

300g plain flour

1 tablespoon baking powder

pinch of salt

¼ teaspoon ground cinnamon

freshly grated nutmeg

175g golden caster sugar

200ml soured cream

2 tablespoons full-fat milk

1 large egg, beaten

100g unsalted butter, melted

finely grated zest of 1 large lemon

1 large Bramley apple, peeled, cored and cut into small pieces

STEP 1

Heat the oven to 200°C/400°F/gas 6. Line a 12-hole muffin tray with paper muffin cases.

STEP 2

Sift the flour, baking powder and salt into a mixing bowl. Stir in the cinnamon, a grating of nutmeg and the sugar. In another smaller bowl, beat together the soured cream, milk, egg, melted butter and lemon zest, just to mix.

STEP 3

Stir the soured cream mixture into the flour and sugar mixture just until evenly combined (it's fine if the mixture is still a bit lumpy). Stir in the apple pieces.

STEP 4

Spoon the mixture into the paper cases, dividing it evenly. Place in the heated oven and bake for 20–25 minutes until risen and golden. Cool for 5 minutes, then serve warm or leave to cool completely before serving.

CORNBREAD

There is something so wholesome and simple about golden cornbread with its crumbly texture and corn-flavoured goodness. Spread it with butter for breakfast, or eat with your pulled pork or Tex-Mex chilli con carne.

MAKES 1 LOAF

YOU WILL NEED: A 1 LITRE OVENPROOF DISH

1 tablespoon olive oil

4 spring onions, both green and white parts, finely sliced

1 green chilli, finely chopped

60g unsalted butter, melted, plus extra for greasing

250g cornmeal or fine polenta, plus extra for dusting

80g plain flour

2 teaspoons baking powder

2 teaspoons salt

1 teaspoon bicarbonate of soda

2 medium eggs

150g full-fat natural yoghurt

200ml full-fat milk

a handful of grated Cheddar cheese

STEP 1

Heat the oil in a frying pan and gently fry the spring onions and chilli for 5–10 minutes until softened. Set aside to cool.

STEP 2

Heat the oven to 220°C/425°F/gas 7. Grease a 1 litre ovenproof dish with butter, then dust with a little cornmeal.

STEP 3

Mix together the cornmeal, flour, baking powder, salt and bicarbonate of soda in a bowl and make a well in the centre. In another bowl, whisk the eggs with the yoghurt, milk and melted butter, then pour into the well in the dry ingredients and mix until thoroughly incorporated. Stir in the spring onions, chilli and cheese, then scoop into the prepared tin.

STEP 4

Place in the heated oven and bake for about 35–40 minutes until golden and starting to come away from the sides of the tin. Serve warm.

SODA BREAD

This might just be the easiest and quickest loaf to make – it doesn't include any yeast, which means there is no kneading and no waiting around for the dough to rise. So when you crave freshly baked bread to eat with your potted shrimps or cheese, or smothered with honey, this bread is the answer.

MAKES 2 LOAVES

400g stoneground wholemeal flour

200g plain white flour, plus extra for dusting

1½ teaspoons salt

1 teaspoon bicarbonate of soda

250ml buttermilk

200ml semi-skimmed milk, plus a little extra for brushing

2 teaspoons runny honey

rolled oats, for sprinkling

STEP 1

Heat the oven to 220°C/425°F/gas 7. Mix together the flours, salt and bicarbonate of soda in a large mixing bowl. Make a well in the centre and pour in the buttermilk, milk and honey, then mix to make a soft, very slightly sticky dough.

STEP 2

Turn out onto a lightly floured worktop and knead lightly until the dough comes together into a ball. Cut in half and knead each piece briefly into a smooth round. Do not over-knead because this will make the bread heavy.

STEP 3

Slightly flatten each round, then place them well apart on a baking sheet lightly dusted with flour. Scatter oats over each loaf. Using a sharp knife, cut a large, deep cross into each loaf, to within about 3cm of the base.

STEP 4

Place on the middle shelf of the heated oven and bake for 15 minutes, then reduce the oven temperature to 200°C/400°F/gas 6. Bake for a further 10–15 minutes until well risen with a golden-brown crust. The loaves should sound hollow when you tap their bases. Leave to cool on a wire rack.

WHITE ROLLS FOR SOUP

The crisp outer shell of these rolls hides a soft centre that is perfect for buttering and dunking into a bowl of steaming soup. If you have time, try a split rise: leave the shaped rolls to rise in a warm place for an hour before removing to the fridge for a further slow rise of a couple of hours. This will make the texture of your rolls even lighter and more tender.

MAKES 12 ROLLS

FOR THE STARTER

120g strong white bread flour

⅛ teaspoon fast-action dried yeast

FOR THE DOUGH

420g strong white bread flour

1½ teaspoons salt

¼ teaspoon fast-action dried yeast

225ml lukewarm water

vegetable oil, for greasing

milk, for brushing

STEP 1

Make the starter the day before. Mix the flour and yeast with 100ml cold water in a large bowl. Cover and leave overnight, at room temperature.

STEP 2

The next day, add the flour for the dough to your starter along with the salt, yeast and lukewarm water. Mix together to form a soft dough. Turn out onto a lightly floured surface and knead for about 10 minutes by hand until the dough is fairly smooth and elastic. Don't worry if it is still a bit sticky.

STEP 3

Shape the dough into a ball and place in a greased bowl. Cover with a tea towel and leave to rise at room temperature for 3 hours – after every hour, knock back the dough in the bowl, then shape it into a ball again.

STEP 4

Turn out the dough onto a lightly greased worktop. Divide into 12 pieces and shape each into a smooth ball. Place on a baking sheet and cover with lightly greased clingfilm. Leave to rise in a warm place for 1–2 hours or in the fridge for 4–5 hours (or overnight). The rolls won't double in size but will be puffy.

STEP 5

If the rolls have been in the fridge, take them out and bring them up to room temperature about 30 minutes before baking. Heat the oven to 210°C/425°F/gas 7. Brush the rolls with milk and slash a cut across the top of each one with a very sharp knife. Place in the heated oven and bake for 20–25 minutes until they are a dark golden colour and crusty. Turn off the oven and open the oven door, then leave the rolls inside to cool.

SOURDOUGH STARTER

There are many methods of making sourdough. To some extent it's a trial and error process to find what works for you, and it can become something of an obsessive labour of love. Your carefully tended starter will respond differently at different times of the year, depending on temperature and humidity, water, yeasts naturally circulating in the air and the type of flour you use – think of it like a pet that needs love and understanding.

One of the beautiful things about sourdough is that those who love it and love making it always want to share, so if you know someone who has a starter, it will be easy to get some to grow yourself. However, if you want to start from scratch, the recipe here will explain how to make your own starter and, from there, your sourdough bread. Be patient and you will reap the rewards. Once you have sourdough mastered you will be addicted for life, and will probably go on to read around the subject and to learn as much as you can about the ways and whims of sourdough bread.

A sourdough starter is as simple as flour and water, but they should both be measured by weight.

FOR STAGE 1

75g strong unrefined bread flour

75g tap water

FOR EACH 'FEED'

75g strong unrefined bread flour

75g tap water

STEP 1

For stage 1, mix the flour and water together in a container. Use your fingers rather than a spoon because you may have natural yeasts on your skin that will add to a good starter. Cover loosely with a lid (don't seal the container because you want the air to get into it – it is the natural yeasts present in the air as well as in the flour that will make your starter live and grow).

STEP 2

The next step is patience. Leave the starter at room temperature for 12 hours, then check if it has started to bubble. If not, wait another 12 hours. If after 36 hours nothing has happened it may be that no natural yeast has cultivated your starter. In this case you need to start again, maybe trying a different flour or putting the container in a different place.

STEP 3

Once your starter is bubbling, it is time to feed it. Add another 75g flour and 75g water and mix with the starter, then cover loosely and leave for 12–24 hours until it begins to bubble once more. It is now time to feed it again in the same way, with 75g flour and 75g water.

STEP 4

When you have reached this point, with your starter growing in size between feeds, you are ready for the next stage. When your starter starts to bubble again, discard roughly half of it, then feed the remainder with 75g flour and 75g water. (If you don't discard some of your starter each time from now on, you will end up with a *lot* of starter. It may seem wasteful, but later on you will use your discard to make bread, or you can give it to friends to start their own sourdough journey.)

STEP 5

You now need to keep feeding your starter every day in this way, discarding half each time, until it is well established (some bakers feed twice a day). Most sourdough bakers recommend that you not use a starter for making bread until it is at least a week old, and that it is best to wait for the starter to be able to roughly double in size between feedings. This could take a month or more!

STEP 6

Once your starter is well established and you are using it to make bread, you can then decide whether you want to keep the starter at room temperature, discarding half and feeding daily, or if you want to keep it in the fridge. The latter slows down the yeast production and sends your starter to sleep, so you don't have to tend to it every day. When you are ready to make bread, take your starter out of the fridge, bring it to room temperature and feed it at least once to make sure it is alive and vigorous before using.

SOURDOUGH BREAD

Once you become familiar with your starter's ways you will soon learn how long it takes to reach its peak after feeding, and to recognise when it has peaked – when it is at its most voluminous and has doubled in size. Just at this point, as it reaches its maximum growth, before it starts to collapse back in a state of exhaustion, is when it is most active and is the best time to use it to make bread.

The amount of starter you use to make your loaf is up to you, and you can experiment with more or less depending on how active your starter is and how strong it is tasting. A good rule of thumb is to use 180–240g of your starter for 500g of bread flour.

MAKES 1 LARGE LOAF

YOU WILL NEED: A PROVING BASKET OR PLASTIC BOX LINED WITH A TEA TOWEL; A PIZZA STONE OR BAKING SHEET; A BAKER'S LAME OR VERY SHARP KNIFE

500g strong white bread flour (or you can try a mix of flours such as rye or wholemeal), plus extra for dusting

180–240g active Sourdough Starter (see pages 262–63)

250–300ml lukewarm water

2 teaspoons salt mixed with 2 teaspoons water

STEP 1
Place the flour in a large bowl and add the starter. Mix with your hands, adding enough lukewarm water to bring the ingredients together into a fairly wet and shaggy-looking dough (the amount of water you need will vary from loaf to loaf). The dough will feel sticky but shouldn't be overly soggy. Leave to rest in the bowl for 10 minutes.

STEP 2
Add the salty water and mix into the dough with your hands. Now wet your hands and knead (in the bowl): stretch the dough away from you, then fold it back on itself. Give the bowl a quarter turn and repeat. Do this for 10 seconds. Leave to rest for 15 minutes, then knead for 10 seconds. Leave for a further 15 minutes and knead once more. Cover the bowl with clingfilm or a tea towel.

STEP 3
Now comes the waiting. You need to leave your dough in a warm place – a warm room is ideal, about 18–20°C – so it will start to rise. The warmth of the room and how active your starter is will affect how long you need to wait. The dough may not double in size like one made with traditional fast-action or fresh yeast, but it will increase by at least half its original volume. This could take anything up to 5 or 6 hours.

STEP 4
Carefully scoop the risen soft dough onto a lightly floured worktop and, with your hands, gently stretch out away from you into a long rectangle. Fold the top third of the rectangle down and

then the bottom third up over it, a bit like folding a business letter for an envelope. Press out the folded dough gently into a long rectangle again. Repeat the folding and pressing out process 2 more times, then form the dough into a smooth round loaf or a boat-shaped loaf.

STEP 5
Place your loaf in a proving basket. (If you don't have a proving basket, a plastic box lined with a flour-dusted tea towel is good.) Cover with clingfilm or a tea towel and leave in a warm place until the loaf has increased by at least half its volume again. This could take a few hours. At this stage, if you don't want to bake straightaway, you can leave your shaped loaf in the fridge overnight; remove it a couple of hours before baking to allow the loaf to come back to room temperature.

STEP 6
When ready to bake, place a pizza stone or baking sheet in the oven and heat it to 230°C/450°F/gas 8. Turn your bread out onto a floured baking sheet. Using a baker's lame or very sharp knife, slice a pattern on the top of your loaf, perhaps cutting a square if you have a round loaf or a long arch for a boat-shaped loaf.

STEP 7
Slide the bread from the floured baking sheet onto the heated pizza stone. Bake for 10 minutes, then reduce the oven to 210°C/410°F/gas 6½. Bake for a further 20–25 minutes until the loaf is golden and risen and sounds hollow when tapped on the base. Cool on a wire rack.

BANANA AND CHOCOLATE LOAF

This seems to sit somewhere in between a cake and a bread, being perfect with a cuppa at teatime or eaten at breakfast as you would a pastry or toast. Whenever you eat it, you'll find that it is utterly delicious. Use really ripe bananas, verging on black, as they will give a lot of flavour to the loaf.

SERVES 6–8

YOU WILL NEED: A 2 LITRE (1KG) LOAF TIN; A HAND-HELD ELECTRIC MIXER

150g unsalted butter, softened, plus extra for greasing

300g plain flour, plus extra for dusting

125g light soft brown sugar

60g dark muscovado sugar

2 large eggs, beaten

1 teaspoon bicarbonate of soda

pinch of salt

150ml soured cream

3 medium-sized ripe bananas

60g dark chocolate (50% cocoa solids), finely chopped

70g pecans, chopped

STEP 1

Heat the oven to 180°C/350°F/gas 4. Lightly grease a 2 litre (1kg) loaf tin with butter, then dust it with flour. Set aside.

STEP 2

Beat the butter with the light brown and muscovado sugars in a bowl with a hand-held electric mixer for 4–5 minutes until really light and fluffy. Gradually add the eggs, beating all the time. Sift in the flour, bicarbonate of soda and salt. Beat well to incorporate, then gradually add the soured cream to make a mixture that will drop off a spoon when it is gently shaken.

STEP 3

Mash the bananas with a fork, then stir them into the mixture along with the chopped chocolate and pecans. Spoon the mixture into the loaf tin and level the top.

STEP 4

Place in the heated oven and bake for about 1 hour until a skewer inserted in the middle of the loaf comes out clean (it may have some chocolate on it if you've pierced through a chocolatey bit). Cover the top with foil if it starts to brown too quickly during baking.

STEP 5

Remove from the oven and allow to cool in the tin for 15 minutes before turning out onto a wire rack to cool completely. Store wrapped in foil or in an airtight tin.

STICKY GINGERBREAD

The gingerbread here is not the sort that you make into people-shaped biscuits, but the dark treacly cake type with a good fiery kick of ginger. The best thing about it is that it gets better with keeping. So if you can resist eating it straightaway, it will mellow in flavour and become even more densely sticky.

SERVES 10–12

YOU WILL NEED: A 2 LITRE (1KG) LOAF TIN

150g unsalted butter, plus extra for greasing

150g dark soft brown sugar

125g golden syrup

125g black treacle

200ml full-fat milk

250g plain flour

2 teaspoons ground ginger

1 teaspoon ground cinnamon

1½ teaspoons baking powder

2 large eggs, beaten

3 pieces of stem ginger in syrup, chopped

STEP 1

Heat the oven to 160°C/325°F/gas 3. Grease a 2 litre (1kg) loaf tin with butter, then line the base and sides with baking paper. Put the butter, sugar, golden syrup and treacle in a small saucepan and heat gently until melted and smooth. Stir in the milk, then set aside to cool.

STEP 2

Sift the flour, ground spices and baking powder into a bowl. Make a well in the centre and pour in the cooled syrup mixture. With a wooden spoon, slowly incorporate the flour mixture, using a circular motion as you would for making a batter. Mix in the beaten eggs and stem ginger.

STEP 3

Pour the mixture into the prepared loaf tin. Place in the heated oven and bake for 50–60 minutes until a skewer inserted in the centre comes out clean. Cool in the tin for 5 minutes, then turn out onto a wire rack to cool completely. If possible, keep in an airtight tin overnight before cutting.

CHILLI AND PINEAPPLE CAKE

Pineapple and chilli are made for each other, with the warmth and flavour of the chilli complementing the sweet fragrance of the pineapple. They work well in this light, tender cake. Serve it as a pud with a dollop of crème fraîche or a scoop of vanilla ice cream.

SERVES 8–10

YOU WILL NEED: 1 X 23CM ROUND DEEP CAKE TIN, GREASED AND LINED WITH BAKING PAPER; A HAND-HELD ELECTRIC MIXER

225g unsalted butter, softened, plus extra for greasing

1 x 567g tin pineapple rings, drained, plus 1–2 tablespoons juice from the tin

225g caster sugar

4 large eggs

200g self-raising flour

50g ground almonds

FOR THE SYRUP

200g caster sugar

1 red chilli, deseeded and finely chopped

grated zest of 1 lime

juice of 4 limes

STEP 1
Heat the oven to 180°C/350°F/gas 4. First make the syrup. Put the sugar, chilli and lime zest and juice in a small saucepan and gently heat until the sugar has dissolved. Increase the heat a bit and bubble gently until the mixture forms a light syrup (it should feel like Vaseline when you rub it between your fingers).

STEP 2
Pour half the chilli syrup into the prepared cake tin and tilt the tin to spread the syrup evenly over the base. Arrange 7 of the pineapple rings on the base, in a single layer. Save the rest of the syrup to pour over the cake later.

STEP 3
Beat the butter and sugar together in a large bowl with a hand-held electric mixer until the mixture is pale and fluffy. Add the eggs, one at a time, beating well until combined. Gently fold in the flour, almonds and enough pineapple juice to give a smooth consistency. Chop the remaining pineapple and fold into the mixture.

STEP 4
Spoon the cake mixture into the tin over the pineapple rings. Place in the heated oven and bake for 45–55 minutes until golden and a skewer inserted into the centre comes out clean. (If the cake is getting a bit too brown during baking, cover with a sheet of baking paper.)

STEP 5
Carefully turn out the cake, upside-down, onto a large serving plate. Warm the remaining chilli syrup and pour over the cake. Cut into slices and serve warm or at room temperature.

MALT LOAF

A slice of rich, sticky, dense malt loaf, smothered in butter, is one of the best indulgences there is. If you can bear to wait to eat it, the flavour will be improved by allowing it to mature, well wrapped, for a few days.

CUTS INTO 12–15 SLICES

YOU WILL NEED: 1 X 900G LOAF TIN

250g mixed sultanas and raisins

200ml just-made tea (without milk)

190g malt extract, plus extra for glazing

butter, for greasing

80g dark brown muscovado sugar

2 medium eggs, beaten

250g plain flour

1 teaspoon baking powder

½ teaspoon bicarbonate of soda

STEP 1

Put the fruit in a bowl. Pour the warm tea over the fruit together with a tablespoon of the malt extract and leave to soak for 1–2 hours.

STEP 2

Heat the oven to 150°C/300°F/gas 2. Grease a 900g loaf tin with butter and line with baking paper. Add the rest of the malt extract and the sugar to the fruit, then beat in the eggs. Stir in the remaining ingredients. Pour into the prepared tin.

STEP 3

Place in the heated oven and bake for 1¼–1½ hours until risen and firm to the touch. Brush with more malt extract, then leave to cool in the tin before turning out.

TEA CAKES

Say 'tea cakes' and what springs to mind is an image of toasting them to a golden brown in front of an open fire. There is truly nothing more cosy than a buttered toasted tea cake.

MAKES 12 TEA CAKES

about 250ml semi-skimmed milk

100ml water

15g fresh yeast OR 1 x 7g sachet fast-action dried yeast

50g unsalted butter, softened

500g strong white bread flour

2 teaspoons salt

1 teaspoon each ground ginger and cinnamon

½ teaspoon each ground cloves and grated nutmeg

40g caster sugar plus 2 tablespoons for the glaze

1 medium egg, beaten

grated zest of 1 lemon

200g mixed raisins and sultanas

35g chopped mixed candied peel

vegetable oil, for greasing

STEP 1

Heat the milk and water in a pan until lukewarm. If using fresh yeast, pour 50ml of the warm liquid into a small bowl and whisk in the yeast until dissolved, then set aside until it froths. Add the butter to the remaining warm liquid and allow it to melt. Sift the flour, salt and spices into a bowl and sprinkle over the dried yeast, if using. Make a well in the centre. Add the fresh yeast mixture (if using), the sugar, egg, lemon zest and the dried fruit and peel. Mix well together, then gradually add the warm buttery liquid, stirring with your fingers until you have a soft, quite sticky dough.

STEP 2

Turn out the dough onto a lightly floured worktop and knead for 10 minutes until smooth and elastic. Shape into a ball. Place in a lightly oiled bowl, cover with clingfilm or a tea towel and leave in a warm place to rise for 1–1½ hours until doubled in size.

STEP 3

Turn out the dough onto the lightly floured worktop and knock back. Divide into 12 equal portions and roll each one into a ball. Flatten each ball to about 1cm thick. Place them, spaced well apart, on a lightly oiled baking sheet and cover with oiled clingfilm. Leave in a warm place to rise for about 40 minutes until doubled in size.

STEP 4

Heat the oven to 200°C/400°F/gas 6. Uncover the tea cakes, then place in the heated oven and bake for 15–20 minutes until golden. Meanwhile, make a glaze by dissolving the extra sugar in 50ml water. Remove the tea cakes from the oven and brush the glaze over them. Cool on a wire rack.

RICH FRUIT CAKE

*A really fruity, dark and moist fruit cake is
so delicious that it is a shame to eat it only at
Christmas or weddings. This one is packed
full of heady spices and nuttiness. You can
cover it with marzipan and icing for the
full Christmas effect or serve it unadorned,
beautifully simple but full of Christmas cheer.*

CUTS INTO 30 SLICES

YOU WILL NEED: A 20CM ROUND, DEEP CAKE TIN;
AN ELECTRIC MIXER

700g mixed currants, raisins and sultanas

6 tablespoons brandy, plus extra for feeding

250g unsalted butter, softened, plus extra for greasing

250g self-raising flour

½ teaspoon salt

1 tablespoon ground mixed spice

1 teaspoon each ground cinnamon and ground ginger

¼ teaspoon each grated nutmeg and ground cloves

150g each glacé cherries and mixed candied citrus peel

150g blanched (skinned) almonds, roughly chopped

170g dark soft brown sugar

grated zest of 1 orange and 1 lemon

4 large eggs

a small splash of milk (optional)

STEP 1

Place the dried fruit in a bowl. Heat the brandy in
a small pan, then pour over the dried fruit. Leave
for an hour or so to absorb the liquid.

STEP 2

Heat the oven to 150°C/300°F/gas 2. Grease
a 20cm round, deep cake tin thoroughly with
melted butter, then line with a double layer of
baking paper that rises 10–12cm above the rim.
Brush the inside of this paper collar generously
with melted butter. Tie a double layer of baking
paper around the outside of the tin, also rising
10–12cm above the rim.

STEP 3

Sift the flour, salt and spices into a large bowl.
Add the soaked fruit, glacé cherries, candied peel
and chopped almonds. Mix together well.

STEP 4

In a separate bowl, cream the butter with the
sugar and orange and lemon zests using an
electric mixer for 4–5 minutes until light and
fluffy. Beat in the eggs one at a time. Stir this
mixture into the flour and fruit. The mixture
should be soft enough to drop off the spoon
when it is gently shaken. If the mix is a little
thick, add a small splash of milk.

STEP 5

Dollop the mixture into the tin. Make a slight indentation in the centre to allow for any rising, then place in the heated oven on the bottom shelf and bake for 1 hour. Reduce the oven temperature to 120°C/250°F/gas ½ and bake for a further 3¼–3½ hours. About 2 hours before the end of the baking time, cover loosely with baking paper to prevent the cake from becoming too dark. The cake is done when it has shrunk a little from the sides of the tin and a skewer inserted into the centre comes out clean.

STEP 6

Remove from the oven and allow to cool a little in the tin before turning out onto a wire rack. Prick the top all over with a skewer, then drizzle over a tablespoon of brandy. Once cold, the cake can be kept, wrapped in clean baking paper and foil or in an airtight tin, for many weeks, and you can feed it regularly with small amounts of brandy.

POPPYSEED TEAR-AND-SHARE LOAF

This bread has a soft white crumb, which makes it ideal for smearing thickly with butter and dunking into soup. Bring the loaf, still warm from the oven, to the table and let people help themselves, pulling the crust apart to get to the soft centre.

MAKES 1 LOAF

200g strong white bread flour, plus extra for dusting

300g plain flour

2 teaspoons salt

15g fresh yeast OR 1 x 7g sachet fast-action dried yeast

300ml semi-skimmed milk, warmed until tepid

50g butter, softened

½ teaspoon caster sugar

1 medium egg

25g poppyseeds, plus extra for sprinkling

beaten egg, for glazing

STEP 1

Sift the bread and plain flours and salt into a mixing bowl. If using fresh yeast, mix it with 50ml of the warmed milk and leave for 10 minutes; if using dried yeast sprinkle it over the flour.

STEP 2

Make a well in the centre of the dry ingredients and add the butter, sugar, egg and fresh yeast mixture, if using. Gradually bring the ingredients together using a wooden spoon, adding the remaining warm milk a little at a time until you have a soft, quite wet dough.

STEP 3

Lightly dust the worktop with flour, then turn out the dough and knead well for 10–15 minutes until smooth and elastic. Transfer to a lightly oiled bowl and cover with a tea towel, then leave in a warm place to rise for an hour until the dough has doubled in size.

STEP 4

Knock back the dough, then knead in the poppyseeds. Remove a third of the dough, shape it into a smooth ball and place it on a greased baking sheet. Divide the remaining dough into 9 equal-sized balls and place them around the larger ball, almost but not quite touching. Cover with a tea towel or lightly greased clingfilm, then leave in a warm place to rise for 45–60 minutes until doubled in size.

STEP 5

Heat the oven to 200°C/400°F/gas 6. Brush the loaf all over with beaten egg and sprinkle a few extra poppyseeds over the surface. Place in the heated oven and bake for 20–25 minutes until risen and golden. Transfer to a wire rack to cool.

HOME-MADE PIZZAS

Whatever floats your boat in terms of toppings – be it a plain and simple margharita, spicy pepperoni or tropical Hawaiian ham and pineapple – the statisfaction of making your own pizza dough is immense. It is so simple and quick enough to make after work. If you are short of baking sheets just shape and cook the pizzas one at a time.

MAKES 2 LARGE PIZZAS

YOU WILL NEED: 2 BAKING SHEETS TO FIT PIZZAS ABOUT 27CM IN DIAMETER

FOR THE PIZZA BASES

250g strong white bread flour, plus extra for dusting

½ teaspoon salt

1 teaspoon caster sugar

1 x 7g sachet fast-action dried yeast

2 teaspoons olive oil, plus extra for greasing

150ml lukewarm water

FOR THE SAUCE

4 tablespoons olive oil

1 onion, finely chopped

3 garlic cloves, finely sliced

2 x 400g tins chopped tomatoes

4 tablespoons tomato purée

leaves picked from a few sprigs of fresh oregano

salt and black pepper

FOR THE TOPPING

toppings of your choice, such as mozzarella cheese, salamis, olives, marinated artichokes and so on

fresh basil leaves

freshly grated Parmesan cheese

STEP 1

Sift the flour and salt into a large bowl, then stir in the sugar and yeast. Make a well in the centre and pour in the oil and a little of the water. With lightly oiled hands, gradually mix the flour into the liquid, adding more water a little at a time, until the ingredients come together into a soft dough. (You may not need all the water.)

STEP 2

Tip out the dough onto a lightly floured worktop, scraping out any dough that sticks to the bowl. Knead the dough for about 10 minutes until it is smooth and supple. Shape it into a ball, put it in a lightly oiled bowl and cover with a tea towel. Leave in a warm place to rise for about an hour until doubled in size.

STEP 3

To make the sauce, heat the oil in a sauté pan over a low heat, then gently fry the onion for 10 minutes until softened. Add the garlic and fry for a further 30 seconds. Add the tinned tomatoes, tomato purée and oregano, and season well with salt and pepper. Cook, stirring occasionally, for 30 minutes until the sauce is thick. You can sieve the sauce if you want it to be really smooth.

STEP 4

Heat the oven, with 2 baking sheets inside, to its highest temperature. Gently knock the air out of the dough, then divide in half. Knead each piece briefly on a lightly floured worktop, then, rolling and pulling gently with your hands, stretch it out to about a 27cm round (or square, oval or other shape). Don't worry if the pizza bases are a bit misshapen. Lay each base on a sheet of baking paper.

STEP 5

Spread 2 tablespoons of the tomato sauce over each base, then add your chosen toppings. Lift the pizzas, on their baking paper, and place on the heated baking sheets in the oven. Bake for about 10–12 minutes until the bases are crisp. Scatter basil leaves and Parmesan over the top, then serve.

SPICED CARROT RELISH ... CRAB
APPLE JELLY ... APPLE AND SULTANA
CHUTNEY ... SEVILLE ORANGE
MARMALADE ... PICCALILLI ...
RHUBARB AND GINGER JAM

PRESERVES & PICKLES

Preserving might seem more appropriate for summer and early autumn fruits and vegetables, but those that arrive in winter — cranberries, crab apples, forced rhubarb and Seville oranges — make sensational preserves.

A proper jam should have quite a firm set but still be spreadable and sweet while allowing the flavour of the fruit to shine through. Fruits and vegetables preserved in vinegar — in chutneys, relishes and pickles — are very welcome on the table at this time of year.

Chutneys, relishes and pickles are very similar, but there are slight differences between them. A chutney is a jumbled mix of chopped fruits, vegetables and dried fruit, cooked slowly with vinegar, sugar and spices until dense and sticky. A relish tends to showcase a single fruit or vegetable. A pickle is normally made with whole or large pieces of fruit and vegetables that have been brined and then preserved in vinegar; the texture is crisper and the flavour more tangy than a chutney or relish.

SPICED CARROT RELISH

An unusual relish to bring to the table with your cheeseboard, this is wonderfully orange and it packs a bit of a ginger-chilli punch. You could also try stirring a good dollop of it through some Greek yoghurt to make a dip for tortilla chips or crisps.

MAKES 6 JARS

YOU WILL NEED: 6 X 450G JARS WITH VINEGAR-PROOF LIDS, STERILISED (SEE PAGE 287)

2 tablespoons yellow mustard seeds

2 tablespoons coriander seeds

2kg carrots, coarsely grated

100g fresh root ginger, peeled and grated

grated zest and juice of 1 lemon

4–5 red chillies, deseeded and very finely sliced

3 cinnamon sticks

2 star anise

2 bulbs of garlic, cloves separated, peeled and gently bashed with a rolling pin

800ml malt vinegar

500ml water

1kg granulated sugar

200g light soft brown sugar

50g flaky sea salt

STEP 1

Put the mustard and coriander seeds in a dry frying pan over a low heat and toast until the mustard seeds start to pop. Roughly crush the seeds in a pestle and mortar, then tip into a large bowl. Add the carrots, ginger, lemon zest and juice, chillies, cinnamon, star anise, garlic and vinegar. Cover and leave to macerate overnight.

STEP 2

Pour the mixture into a large heavy-based saucepan or preserving pan and add the water, granulated and brown sugars and the salt. Set the pan over a low heat and cook, stirring constantly, until the sugar has dissolved. Increase the heat and boil the mixture for 30–40 minutes until it starts to become jammy.

STEP 3

Remove from the heat and spoon the hot relish into 6 sterilised 450g jars. Seal and allow to cool. The relish is ready to eat straight away, but it will keep in a cool, dark place for 6–8 months.

CRAB APPLE JELLY

Jars of clear, rosy crab apple jelly are a beautiful sight to behold – line them up on your windowsill and watch the winter sun sparkle through them. Not only is crab apple jelly delicious as a condiment with roast meats such as pork or pheasant, but it is also great stirred in little dollops into gravy to give sweetness or served with cheese and cold meats. If you have never tried spreading crab apple jelly on hot buttered toast you are missing out on a tasty delight.

MAKES 6 JARS

YOU WILL NEED: A JELLY BAG OR MUSLIN; 6 X 450G JARS WITH LIDS, STERILISED (SEE OPPOSITE)

3–4kg crab apples

about 1kg granulated sugar

pared zest of 1 lemon

STEP 1

Wash the crab apples and cut out any bruises or damaged parts. Place in a large heavy-based saucepan or preserving pan and pour in enough cold water to barely cover them. Bring to the boil, then simmer until the whole mass of fruit has become a pulpy mush, squishing the fruit against the side of the pan from time to time.

STEP 2

Tip the mixture into a jelly bag suspended over a very large bowl. (If you don't have a jelly bag, line a very large bowl with a big square of muslin; pour in the pulp, then bring the sides and corners of the muslin up around the fruit pulp to make a bag and tie together. Suspend over the bowl.) Allow the juice to drain from the pulp into the bowl overnight; do not squeeze the bag or muslin or your jelly will be cloudy, not clear.

STEP 3

The next day, measure how much juice you have. For every 1 litre of juice you will need 700g of granulated sugar. Combine the juice with the sugar in a clean saucepan or preserving pan and add the lemon zest. Set the pan over a low heat and stir until the sugar has dissolved.

STEP 4

Increase the heat and bring to the boil, then boil rapidly for up to 40 minutes, skimming off any scum that rises to the surface.

STEP 5

Start testing the jelly regularly for setting point after it has been boiling for about 10 minutes. If you are using a thermometer you want the mixture to reach 106°C. To test for setting point without a thermometer, spoon a little of the mixture onto a plate and cool in the fridge for a couple of minutes: if a thick skin has formed and the surface wrinkles when you push your finger through the mixture, then you've reached setting point. If not, continue boiling and test again after 5 minutes.

STEP 6

Once setting point has been reached, remove from the heat and ladle into 6 warm, sterilised 450g jars. Top each with a disc of waxed paper and a lid, then leave until cold. Store in a cool, dark place for a few weeks before eating. The jelly will keep for up to a year.

STERILISING JARS AND BOTTLES

Heat the oven to 140°C/275°F/gas 1. Wash the jars or bottles and their lids in warm soapy water, then rinse with clean, hot water. Turn jars upside down, or bottles on their sides, on a clean baking sheet and place in the heated oven to dry for 10 minutes. Use a clean cloth to handle the hot jars and bottles.

Alternatively, you can run the jars and bottles through the hot cycle of the dishwasher.

APPLE AND SULTANA CHUTNEY

Everyone needs a good recipe for an apple chutney to eat with cheese. It is the staple of the chutney world. The chutney here is robust and tangy, with a mellow hint of mustard seeds and juicy plump sultanas.

MAKES 6–8 JARS

YOU WILL NEED: 6–8 X 450G JARS WITH VINEGAR-PROOF LIDS, STERILISED (SEE PAGE 287)

2 tablespoons vegetable oil

3 tablespoons black mustard seeds

1 tablespoon fenugreek seeds

2 teaspoons ground ginger

2 large onions, finely chopped

2kg Bramley apples, peeled, cored and cut into small chunks

500g sultanas

1 tablespoon salt

600g light soft brown sugar

750ml malt or cider vinegar OR a mix of the two

STEP 1

Heat the oil in a large heavy-based saucepan or preserving pan and fry the black mustard seeds and fenugreek seeds until they start to pop. Stir in the ground ginger and onion and cook for 5 minutes until the onion is softened.

STEP 2

Add the rest of the ingredients and cook over a low heat until the sugar has dissolved, then bring to the boil. Reduce the heat again and simmer for 1–1½ hours until thickened.

STEP 3

Remove from the heat, then spoon the chutney into 6–8 sterilised 450g jars and seal. Set aside to cool completely. Leave to mature in a cool, dark place for a few weeks before eating. The chutney will keep for up to a year.

SEVILLE ORANGE MARMALADE

Seville oranges have a really short season that is eagerly anticipated by marmalade-makers all winter. This is because the oranges have a thick skin that gives a distinctively bitter but rich flavour to marmalade. It is up to you how thick or thin you want the shreds of peel in your marmalade to be.

MAKES 6 JARS

YOU WILL NEED: MUSLIN; 6 X 450G JARS WITH LIDS, STERILISED (SEE PAGE 287)

1kg Seville oranges

2.5 litres cold water

1.7kg preserving sugar

juice of 2 large lemons

STEP 1

Cut the oranges in half and squeeze all the juice into a large bowl; reserve the pips. Add the cold water to the juice. Remove the pulp from the inside of the oranges and reserve with the pips.

STEP 2

Shred the orange peel into strips – thin or thick. Add to the bowl, then cover and leave in a cool place overnight.

STEP 3

Pour the juice mixture into a large heavy-based saucepan or preserving pan. Tie the reserved pulp and pips in a muslin bag and submerge this in the liquid. Bring to the boil, then reduce to a simmer and cook gently for 1½–2 hours until the peel is translucent and tender.

STEP 4

Remove the muslin bag, squeezing as much liquid as possible from it back into the pan. Add the sugar and lemon juice and allow the sugar to dissolve over a low heat. Once it has dissolved, increase the heat and boil rapidly for up to 50 minutes, skimming off any scum that rises to the surface.

STEP 5

After 15 minutes of boiling you can start to test for a set. If you are using a thermometer you want the mixture to reach 106°C. To test for setting point without a thermometer, spoon a little of the mixture onto a plate and cool in the fridge for a couple of minutes: if a thick skin has formed and the surface wrinkles when you push your finger through the mixture, then you've reached setting point. If not, continue boiling and test every 5 minutes or so.

STEP 6

Remove from the heat and leave to settle for 10 minutes, skimming off any scum that rises to the surface, then ladle the marmalade into your 6 sterilised jars. Top each with a waxed disc and seal with a lid. Cool completely. The marmalade will keep in a cool, dark place for several years.

PICCALILLI

Here is an autumnal version of piccalilli. It can be eaten immediately, but will taste even better if left to mature for a few months.

MAKES 6–8 JARS

YOU WILL NEED: 6–8 X 450G JARS WITH VINEGAR-PROOF LIDS, STERILISED (SEE PAGE 287)

150g salt

2.5 litres cold water

600g cauliflower, broken into small florets

200g carrots, cut into small dice

1 large cucumber, deseeded and cut into small pieces

200g little shallots, quartered

4 firm pears, cored and cut into small chunks

1 litre cider vinegar

200g caster sugar

1 garlic clove, crushed

5cm piece fresh root ginger, peeled and grated

60g cornflour

2 tablespoons each mustard powder and turmeric

1 teaspoon ground ginger

1 tablespoon each of yellow mustard and coriander seeds

½ teaspoon crushed dried chilli

STEP 1

Dissolve the salt in the water. Put the cauliflower and carrots into a bowl, and the cucumber, shallots and pears into a second bowl. Divide the salted water between the bowls. Leave overnight.

STEP 2

The following day, drain and rinse the vegetables and pears, keeping the 2 batches separate. Put the vinegar, sugar, garlic and fresh ginger into a large heavy-based saucepan or preserving pan and bring to the boil, stirring to dissolve the sugar. Add the cauliflower and carrots and cook for 5 minutes, then add the cucumber, shallots and pears and cook for a further 3 minutes until the vegetables are just cooked but still with some crunch left. Remove the vegetables and pears with a slotted spoon and place in a large bowl.

STEP 3

Mix the cornflour, mustard powder, turmeric and ground ginger with 4 tablespoons of the hot vinegar mixture to make a smooth paste. Add this to the rest of the vinegar in the pan, along with the mustard seeds, coriander seeds and crushed chilli flakes. Bring to the boil, stirring, then simmer for 2 minutes until the sauce is thick.

STEP 4

Stir the sauce into the vegetables to coat evenly. Spoon into 6 warm, sterilised 450g jars, cover with waxed discs and seal with lids. Leave to cool. The pickle can be kept in a cool, dark place for up to a year.

RHUBARB AND GINGER JAM

The first rhubarb of the season is forced (grown in the dark), which gives it its beautiful bright pink colour. This rhubarb makes the prettiest jam, a ray of colour in a wintery world. Later on in the year you can use green-stemmed rhubarb, which is less pink but just as delicious. Rhubarb has low natural pectin (the substance found in fruit that causes jams and jellies to set), so you need to add extra pectin or your jam will run off your bread! To make sure the jam sets, use preserving sugar, which has added pectin, and add lemon, which is naturally high in pectin.

MAKES ABOUT 6 JARS

YOU WILL NEED: MUSLIN; 6 X 450G JARS WITH LIDS, STERILISED (SEE PAGE 287)

1.5kg rhubarb

1.5kg preserving sugar

grated zest and juice of 1 lemon

4cm piece fresh root ginger, hit with a rolling pin to squash it a little

125g preserved stem ginger in syrup, drained and finely chopped

STEP 1

Cut the rhubarb into 2.5cm lengths and place in a bowl with the sugar. Toss well to combine, then cover and leave to macerate overnight. The sugar should have mostly dissolved and you should have a syrupy mass.

STEP 2

Scrape this mixture into a large heavy-based saucepan or preserving pan and add the lemon zest and juice. Tie the crushed ginger in a muslin bag (this makes it easier to remove later) and add to the pot. Bring to the boil slowly, then boil vigorously until the rhubarb is breaking down and you have reached setting point.

STEP 3

Start testing the jam regularly for setting point after it has been boiling for about 10 minutes. If you are using a thermometer you want the mixture to reach 106°C. To test without a thermometer, spoon a little of the mixture onto a plate and cool in the fridge for a couple of minutes; if a skin has formed and the surface wrinkles when you push your finger through the mixture, then you've reached setting point. If not, boil for a further 5 minutes and test again.

STEP 4

Once setting point has been reached, remove the bag of ginger and stir through the stem ginger. Ladle the hot jam into 6 warm, sterilised 450g jars. Cover each with a disc of waxed paper and a lid, then leave to cool. The jam will keep in a cool, dark place for up to a year.

INDEX

ACKNOWLEDGEMENTS

BBC Books and Love Productions would like to thank the following people for their invaluable contribution to this book:
Lizzie Kamenetzky, Norma Macmillan, Susanna Cook, Maeve Bargman, Lucy Mahony and Allies Design, Andrew Barron, Nassima Rothacker, Annie Nichols, Polly Webb-Wilson, Abi Waters, Clare Sayer, Marion Moisy, Corinne Masciocchi, Lisa Footit and Sam Beddoes.

ALSO AVAILABLE FROM
THE GREAT BRITISH
BAKE OFF

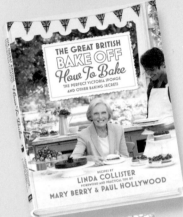

How to achieve baking perfection at home, with foolproof recipes and simple step-by-step masterclasses based on Mary and Paul's Technical Challenges.

Baking doesn't have to be complicated to be 'showstopping'. Inspired by the Showstopper Challenge, here are bakes that will both turn heads and make mouths water.

Simple, reliable, delicious bakes for every day — these are the recipes you will return to over and over again.

Packed with practical advice to help you improve your baking. It includes fascinating trivia covering the history of baking and the chemistry crucial to achieving winning bakes.

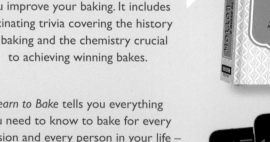

Learn to Bake tells you everything you need to know to bake for every occasion and every person in your life — 80 easy recipes for all the family.

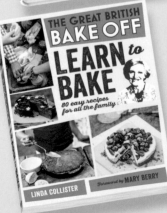

Recipes from your favourite show, now in your pocket! Download *The Great British Bake Off* app and get 60 amazing recipes.